Nick was brought up on an active Thames spritsail barge on the River Medway, Kent. Following training as an engineer officer cadet with the Royal Fleet Auxiliary, he rose through the ranks until medically retired in 1999. Nick married Christobel in 1978 and they soon bought their first boat. Upon leaving the sea, Nick retrained and worked with adults with special needs. During leaves and holiday periods sailing aboard their beloved *Whimbrel* and walking have been jointly enjoyed. Writing about his childhood spawned a series of coastal books. Sailing and 'living' life are his main interests.

SAILING
Through
LIFE...

NICK ARDLEY

Austin Macauley Publishers™
LONDON • CAMBRIDGE • NEW YORK • SHARJAH

A CIP catalogue record for this title is available from the British Library.

ISBN 9781398481336 (Paperback)
ISBN 9781398481343 (Hardback)
ISBN 9781398481350 (ePub e-book)

www.austinmacauley.com

First Published 2023
Austin Macauley Publishers Ltd®
1 Canada Square
Canary Wharf
London
E14 5AA

For all who have sailed aboard Whimbrel, with love...

And especially for my dear mother, who loved the water:

14 December 1931 to 26 December 2021.

Sail on, Mother. Wander the eternal shorelines and wooded glades.
Sit, ponder, and sketch, forever...

God Bless.

First, I must sincerely thank the people who regularly crew with me and have allowed 'their' stories to be told. Most are family members and others who are within the extended family: Graham A, Theresa, Andrew, Roger, Graham D, Hannah and Steve, Paul and, of course, my dear wife (the mate) who is 'aboard' even when not physically so. There are others not specifically mentioned but all have contributed to the richness of life aboard my clinker sloop, Whimbrel.

I need to also thank the Sea Change sailing Trust for the glorious day we had aboard the delightful Blue Mermaid. The day created a tale. We look forward to continuing to support your good work. Thank you, Richard, Hilary, and Ollie.

To all the above people and so many more, I hold you all in deepest regard for the love and support shown during my cancer journey. It made such a huge difference to my wellbeing, and of my immediate family. From the bottom of my heart, thank you, one and all.

Table of Contents

Western Isle of Scotland

Isle of Skye

Canna

Pt of Seat
Knoydart
Mallaig
Inverie
Loch Nevis

Rhum

Eigg

Muck

Ardnamurchan Pt   Loch Sunart

Eileen Mor

Tobermory

Treshnish
Is   Lunga
Staffa Ulva   Isle of Mull

Iona   Eilean-nam-ban

SUFFOLK

R. Alde   Aldeburgh
Snape
Iken

Orford
Butley River
Woodbridge
R. Oare   Orford
Ipswich   Waldringfield   Ness
R.Orwell   Ramsholt
Pinmill   R. Deben
R.Stour
Manningtree   Harwich   Languard Point
Mistley   Pennyhole
Bay
Colchester   Walton
Backwaters   The Naze
R. Colne   Wivenhoe   Walton-on-the-Naze

ESSEX

Brightlingsea   The Wallet

Mersea
Island   Clacton

Tollesbury   Gunfleet
R. Blackwater   Colne Bar   Sands

Maldon   Bradwell   Swatchwatchway

Buxey Sand

Maylandsea   Whitaker Spit

North Fambridge   East Barrow
Burnham

Battlesbridge   R. Crouch   The Swin

R. Roach   West   Thames
Rochford   Foulness Is.   Barrow
Maplin Sands   Estuary
Leigh-on-Sea

Canvey Is.   Southend-on-Sea

River Thames – Sea Reach

Red Sands Towers
The Nore

Isle of   Middle Sands
Grain   Sheerness
R. Medway   Four Fathom   Margate
Upnor   Queenborough   Channel   Sands
Isle of Sheppey
Strood   Gore Channel   North
Chatham   E. Swale   Reculvers   Foreland
Rochester   Lower Halstow   Sarre
Milton   Whitstable   Sandwich   Ramsgate
Conyer   Pegwell Bay
Oare
Faversham   **KENT**

Nick Ardley

Regions covered in Sailing through life.

Preface

Following the publication of my last work, *Rochester to Richmond a Thames Estuary Sailor's View*, I have been asked on numerous occasions by sailors and like-minded people interested in coastal 'goings on' if there was to be another book. One sailor, aboard a swish-looking yacht with deep grey Kevlar sails, racing down the River Medway during a regatta even rose from his position and shouted out as we passed. As the question floated to my ears, I quickly retorted, 'Maybe...' whilst nonchalantly waving.

So, in truth, the 'Maybe...' although not a commitment in my own mind had already been a bundle of kindling splinters flickering in the fireplace for germination of this volume had already taken place. It had initially bubbled and fizzed into headers, jottings and larger pieces of 'scrawl' however, it was set aside with a deep sadness. That was during a personal low point early in the Covid-19 pandemic.

We had received threats after a blog I wrote. This was followed by verbal abuse, alone, out on the water, far from help. For both of us, it was a deeply upsetting and frightening experience and I swore never to share any further words of wisdom from my life of sailing experiences.

As time travelled on, I thought, *why should victims remain silent*...echoing the 'me too...' movement. So, one morning, early in January 2021, whilst in another prolonged lockdown, I settled down and took a close look at what I had. Most was scrapped! I then began with 'a blank sheet' talking about my cancer journey, which was settling out as 'good' after the cessation of treatments. Men, especially, must take heed of this tale.

I was captive, between walks, with time and space. The stories were all floating in my mind. I sought the views of family and friends for their being directly mentioned, talked about and humoured as words rolled and tumbled on the flowing tide. As March 2021 and the lockdown ended, the work was largely completed.

In this volume, I tell the tales in the same fashion as done in my last work. I have not disappeared down the historical path unless I felt it was to be worthy of inclusion. The premise: it must add something. That said, there are two tales where the history of a couple of waterways has long been of interest to me.

The Covid-19 pandemic is writ large throughout. It overlapped my cancer journey. It impinged on sailing in a big way. Events through the period have affected my and my wife's lives, so have been written about too.

Christobel has again loved being the first reader of these tales. She's ably wielded her 'red' pen enabling me to take another look as needed. So, I hope you the reader, will find fresh enjoyment voyaging with the skipper and his mate aboard their beloved clinker sloop *Whimbrel*…

1
Sailing Through Life!

Throughout my time on this wonderful planet, my life has revolved significantly round the water. First, aboard a spritsail barge, the *May Flower*, which was my childhood and adolescent home. Then, I 'ran away' to a seafaring training, which ultimately led me to my college time sweetheart. Sea life, engineering on big ships, with long periods away made for a long engagement.

After gaining an essential promotion qualification, I married my beloved Christobel and our home was set up close to the water. It was an inadvertent choice, I might add: Christobel gained a teaching post at a Church of England school on Canvey Island on the Thames shore of Essex. Working at sea, I could have lived anywhere. Life continued with few cares, during which time I 'enjoyed' 30 years working afloat as an engineer officer, interspersed with my love for sailing.

Bluetail, a Yachting World Peoples Boat was the first boat owned (jointly) aboard which Christobel became 'the mate' and grew to love the rivers, creeks and marshlands of our beloved greater Thames Estuary. Then *Whimbrel* came along. She soon became the joy of my leave periods from deep-sea (and war) experiences. It was upon being medically retired, before my full term was up, that created a firmer bond with 'my' boat. It gave me a release. Since I have sailed aboard *Whimbrel* as often as 'I can get away with it'…that does not mean all else is pushed aside to feed my desire though.

Being 'beached' was the first time in my life that I had to sit and really consider the future. What it meant for me, my dear wife and family to a lesser extent for 'the boy' who was then setting out on his own pathway and our finances and security. For some 12 months I spent many hours carrying out voluntary work at my yacht club – sometimes for up to four days a week. It kept me busy. It helped soothe worries. It gave me a purpose, however briefly.

Then by chance after helping out at my wife's school (you could in those days!) listening to readers, I took up an offer to become an adult learning support assistant. I went back to 'school' working as a volunteer at an adult education college. I fell into working with adult students with learning disabilities – something extremely different to engineering on sea-going ships. I studied and managed to pass a qualification too. I soon found I had a purpose with a lot to offer, again. It was fulfilling.

Sitting at my desk, writing, I remember one glorious morning when based at a teaching annexe not far from where *Whimbrel* is berthed. I popped down to the moorings, prepared the boat for a sail, then shot off to the class. Five minutes after class I was walking round my club's mooring walkways to the boat, by then afloat as well as readied. (There was an aside to that particular sail, written about in *Mudlarking*, when I inadvertently sailed into a patch of saltings, towards highwater!)

Home duties 'took but a trice' and with college taking a mere three mornings a week, *Whimbrel* was always there for me. The little clinker sloop provided a 'happy place' and for that reason, she sits high on my personal agenda. I started writing too, seriously, for although I had occasionally popped the odd article in the post to a yachty mag, within a couple of years of my enforced change in direction, I began writing about my early life aboard the *May Flower,* with everything else that followed.

Heading home on a late December 2017 sail.

I have been blessedly fortunate in that *Whimbrel* is enjoyed by my mate too. So many wives or partners do not follow their men to sea. There is often good reason for that, but I shan't discuss here. Interestingly, Christobel maintains that 'the boat' is most definitely 'the other lady' in my life. My mistress in fact! I can certainly live with that!

A few weeks towards the end of 2017, we both received invitations to attend an appointment at our surgery for a cardio-vascular check. Now, these checks when made, although they perform an essentially vital view of one's health, have never included, in my or my mate's experience, any other interest in our general health. The: How are you? How do you feel? Do you have any other concerns? Etc, etc, have never featured.

It so happened that a little before the surgery visit during the dawn of 2018, I was stopped in my tracks and took immediate notice of an interview taking place on BBC Radio 4. It was between the then senior presenter (now retired) and the National Health Service Chief (of England). The discussion revolved round prostate cancer and the little-known fact that all men from the age of 50 years were entitled to a simple blood test to check for this insidious 'man' disease. It was also stated that deaths from prostate cancer had overtaken those for women (in the main) dying of breast cancer. That took my breath away. I was totally surprised. So, I thought, I'll ask for one.

I had the checks – no questions about general health. Was told to exercise more – 'we' walk up to 40 kilometres a week – which the health worker clearly didn't do: we nick-named her 'butter ball' and I quipped later to Christobel that the two of us could have got inside her skirt! I was told I needed to check my blood pressure for two weeks and come back – I ended up on blood pressure control tablets!

To continue, I said, "I want a PSA test please…"

"What for?" the health worker asked.

"I was entitled from 50…' I said, pausing before adding, "I'm 62 this year…"

"Have you any symptoms?"

"No, I don't think so…" I could feel this getting away from me, so added, "I should have one."

"We don't dish out tests willy-nilly," was the terse response.

So, I banged the desk! "I want one…" I said, with a touch of anger. With flushed cheeks, we looked at each other: I'd shocked both of us.

The health care worker looked down at something or other, probably to gain time, then said, "Excuse me…" and went off to speak to a doctor. On her return, she said, "You're to have some blood tests, so the doctor said to tick the box…" and with a touch of sarcasm added, "for a prostate-specific antigen test," spelling it out. I thanked her and left.

Here lies a warning: don't wait, ask, demand. It is a right. Proper screening would save a huge amount of money downstream. Remember chaps, one is an exceedingly a long time dead!

To cut this short. What a Bloody Good Job I asked: I had a high prostate specific antigen (PSA) reading.

My doctor told me that there wasn't anything to worry about. He said, "It'll be referred to the hospital though…" The import that did not sink in. I went away whistling, metaphorically: I've never mastered the art, with just a tiny worry, buzzing.

Readers can look all of this guff up about this very real problem at their leisure and heed the warnings within this tale by asking themselves, *do I want to live life to the full, or die well before my time…*

During the remainder of that winter and early spring, we both carried on doing normal stuff like, marmalade making, walking, enjoying a couple of day trips to London for exhibitions and a theatre visit. I was sailing as much as possible too. Most important though, we were also getting set to celebrate our Ruby Wedding Anniversary, with a long weekend away covering the day and a further holiday in wonderful Amsterdam.

For added excitement, before the two holidays, I had an Essex Book Festival talk to prepare and deliver, which was a little bit of fun…I had an incredibly good turnout at a South Essex library, which was uplifting indeed.

We had a fabulous time on our 'dirty weekend' which we spent at a little place then called 'The Red Sails' in Faversham. Our week in Amsterdam was also brilliant – we walked almost everywhere and only once took a ride, on a tourist boat round some of the scenic waterways. The Rijks Museum and the Maritime Museum were two particularly memorable highlights.

A couple of 'our' best funny moments was when I caught my good mate looking at tins of 'weed' – she posed for the picture too! This was followed by our inadvertent 'falling into' a 'coffee house' – wrong. As the intoxicating mist enveloped us, we about turned, stumbling over each other's feet and made our escape into a more likely looking café next door, blushing and giggling like a couple of newlyweds!

My mate sampling in Amsterdam!

Returning and with time moving on, I began to plan when we would put *Whimbrel* on the club hard for a scrub and give her a coat of antifouling. I'd also arranged sailing trips with a cousin and my youngest brother – two of the most amenable crewmembers to have aboard. I had also finalised a week-long trip with another 'favourite crew' – my sister and two of her friends, both of whom have become our good friends of ours too.

Then, when I was beginning to think there really wasn't anything to be concerned about, I had a call from the surgery. The hospital to which I was supposedly referred, wasn't happy. I was sent for another blood test. This next test resulted in being called back to the doctor's surgery where I 'enjoyed my first internal' being thoroughly 'reamed out' I thought, Blood Heck!

"All seems fine…" the doctor said, peeling off his gossamer latex gloves. Then smiling, he added, "there doesn't seem to be a problem…" As if to reassure me, continued, "…but a specialist should look…you'll be referred to the hospital." I looked at him, unsmilingly. I felt a chill, as he coldly added, dismissing me, "You'll get a letter…"

I wasn't reassured. I was beginning to feel decidedly fluttery. The thoughts within my head were in the first stages of near frantic worry. Looking back, I think I began to block those thoughts straight away.

Towards the end of May, *Whimbrel* was put on the hard for the mate's most favoured activity – bottom scrub and antifouling. We do the sides on alternate tides, evening and morning…These days we use a pressure washer which makes life easier. I have to say, I don't get a look in after connecting everything up: the mate is like a sword flourishing dervish. My job is to deal with the centre plate pivot bolt, propeller cleaning and checking of hull fittings and pintle strap fastenings. The top sides get a check-over and touch-ups are also done whilst accessible. While my mate coats the major bottom area, I deal with the boot top and cutting in. Hey ho.

The hospital letter came, it was the first of many. My PSA was well above the point when alarm bells would normally have been triggered, had I had an earlier test. It had clearly been rising for some years, probably. The gravity of all of this still did not sink in at all, for the National Heath website and that of another leading Cancer organisation clearly stated that PSA tests were unreliable and often incorrect.

At the hospital, I had another internal from a specialist. He found lumps which he wasn't very happy about down one side of my prostate. "I'll book you for a scan," he said, "it'll be within a week…" My heart leapt. I swear it missed a beat.

I managed to question the oncologist about what the surgery had said and what was on health websites, including NHS site. He said, bluntly, "It's not rocket science, if you have a lump and a high PSA level…there is a problem to be investigated…"

We, for we always went together, left the hospital in less than a jovial mood.

It was now early June. We had a few days away and another period taking in our Finesse Rally which took place at Chatham that year – it was fun meeting many old and new friends. It provided sustenance to my frayed self. The period also took in 'my birthday sail' which did not include our usual visit to Conyer, which had become a custom. We needed to get home for an appointment, but we did get to Conyer before the month was out though.

Life was now being lived round hospital appointments.

So, the day before my scan appointment, we sailed home. The scan was for a localised look at the middle areas surrounding my prostate. This was quickly followed by a day patient visit, the day before Father's Day, for a biopsy operation. In between, I nipped out on the tide for a gentle tranquilising sail!

A follow-up consultation after the biopsy had us walking into a consultation room to see a surgeon. I was not in a good frame of mind. (Christobel accompanied me on all these visits, so I might ding-dong between we and I, mostly I will mean both of us!).

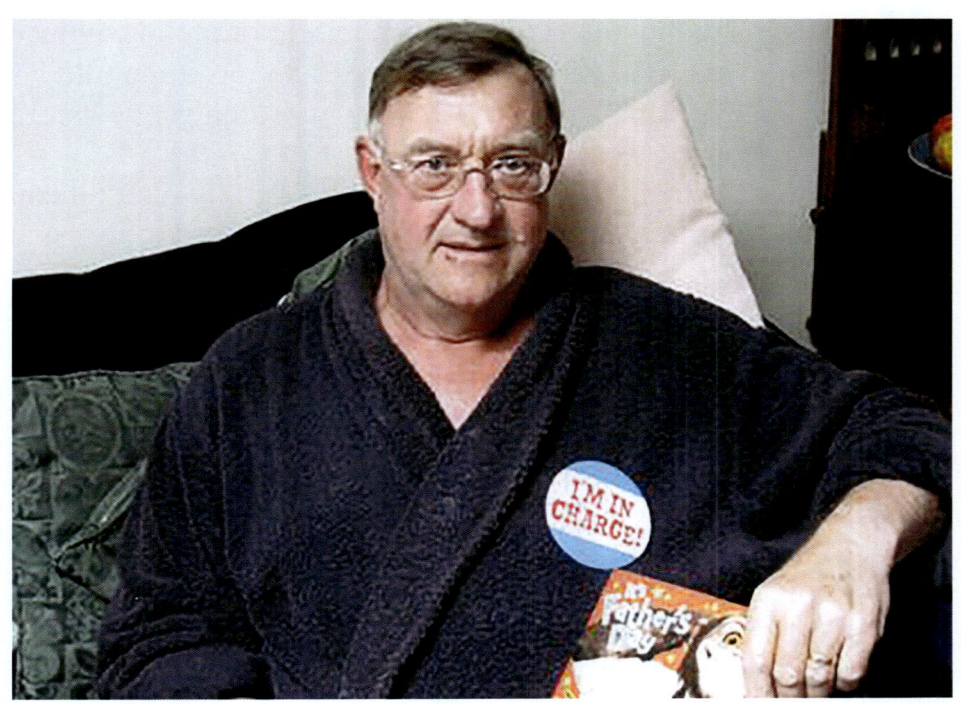

Home after my biopsy.

It was bad news. Words were spoken. I heard them. I shivered. My blood felt chilled. I didn't know what to say. I swallowed hard. Tears were starting to bubble…I looked at Christobel, *Whimbrel's* mate and my all. Our life together was flashing before my rapidly blinking eyes…then a numbness enfolded me. Was this the end of my, our, road?

I was asked, "You do understand…" It seemed bald and bloody pointed.

No. I thought, *I Bloody Well Don't,* but stammered, "Y-es," feeling my hand being gripped ever tighter by my mate sitting close beside me.

"You've got cancer…" the surgeon added gently. Then smiling, he said, "but we'll deal with it."

I remember saying, in a voice shaking with too many emotions, "I'm too young to die…" And I heard a sharp intake of breath from my mate.

"This will not kill you…" the surgeon said, quietly, trying to exude confidence into me, "we can fix it…"

The surgeon didn't allude to what would 'do for me'. I continue to hope that it would be far into the future, with me at the tiller as I sailed through a marshland sun-kissed creek with a gentle breeze caressing my cheek…

I was given several pamphlets and advised to fully digest them. And that was that. We walked out of the room, shocked to the core. Me, clutching those papers, tightly.

I was feeling utterly blank, but aware that the mate was by then in floods of tears. A nurse sat us both down and asked if we would like some tea.

Bloody Tea I thought, silently, as I shook my head, endeavouring to smile back…I was petrified like some trees we'd found on a walk – dead, inside.

As Christobel's tears swelled and spilled down her hot flushed cheeks. All I could do was hold her…"It'll be alright…" I was unbelievably saying: I felt numb too.

Before leaving, I was given an appointment to see a range of people. A specialist nurse, an oncologist and a surgeon within two weeks, but also to come back in a couple of days for a bone scan – a check for any spread through my body: prostate cancer apparently latches onto and attacks bones very quickly.

On the way home, we stopped at a Leigh-on-Sea café, we had been regularly using. I blankly ordered coffees, smoked salmon and cream cheese bagels and a Portuguese custard tart each. We sat outside; it seemed the best place in the circumstances.

It was a clear day. I could see far out across the Thames. From a deeply blue-sky, bright sunshine streamed down, bathing us in the early summer warmth. Christobel's grey nylons shimmered below the blue lace summer skirt she was wearing. The garment had by then become totemic on hospital visits. She was smiling bravely. Her eyes bright, puffed and edge reddened had beaded tears of fright bubbling, every now and then, as we talked. Strange, looking back, how things are remembered.

Arriving home, petrified, I broke down completely. I have to be honest; I fell to pieces: I now realised that my time might be limited. Those sheets of information sat in front of me, blurred and of no real consequence, I felt.

I blindly watched Christobel, as she'd promised, begin the task of ringing the family. I tried to talk to a brother in Canada, but couldn't string any sensible words together, he was consoling. His own wife has had her own cancer fight…

For a couple of days, I was numbed. I kept thinking, *this isn't good*…but also, knew, deep down, that so many other people had travelled this road and had come through…

In time, I read and reread all the reams of 'blurb' and tried to take it all in. It was impossible. I just had a blankness, not wanting to digest anything. There was just too much. The differing types of treatment. The lists of side effects and much more were, in themselves, frightening. I was deeply scared.

I was 'Petrified' like these trees found on a walk.

The appointments spoken about came through, right smack in the middle of a week when I was planning on a sail with my favoured crews. A trip to Upnor, Greenhithe, Limehouse for a night, Erith, Queenborough, Conyer and home. So, the extended family week was cancelled. It hurt, but as my sister said, you've got to go to the appointment. I knew that! Plans weren't all thrown awry though, as I was later to find out.

A bit of relief for me came along with promising weather for a planned sailing trip with a cousin and a brother. Two good, sound and congenial crewmates. We always have a good time. I always tell my crews, 'You're the best…' which they all know they are!

My cousin has always looked forward to the day when he's able to come aboard for a longer sail, but his work at a well-known high-street bank has prevented it thus far. Not so long now, mate!

Our trip was relatively short in miles but superb in quality. The forecast for the period was settled with a high pressure giving generally easterly airflows. A north-easterly should have given us a close reach straight into the mouth of the River Medway, but it was clearly from the east southeast. So, in sparkling sunshine, we cleared my creek's mooring and set about tacking across the Thames highway on the afternoon tide, nattering.

"Sail on…" I said quietly, looking at my brother, as we passed the Queenborough Spit cardinal buoy. Then looking at them both, said, "I'll luff up shortly and we'll clear away the mains'l…"

Not long afterwards, the two crew stowed the mainsail and my brother prepared the mooring line and boathook line. Quietly, we ghosted onto a buoy under jib, moored and tidied ship. Over a beer in the cockpit with some nibbles, I calmly chatted to my crew about my very recent diagnosis, filling in greater detail to the bald facts already made known to the family. No one down the line was thought to have suffered from prostate cancer, we all decided, but I asked both to get checked.

Ashore, the crew was introduced to the newly famous Queenborough hostelry, the Admiral's Arm, where I had picked up on a misspent youth during early pubbing days.

Inside, I said, "Crips and pickled eggs dropped in…" adding, "the beer is good in here too."

"Yes please…" I heard, in response from one but not the other.

The host, smiling in recognition and welcome, soon described the week's ale selection. My cousin declined an egg but like us, was soon quaffing his beer!

The next morning, after a lazy breakfast we departed from our buoy under sail – main and Genoa set – in a friendly north-easterly, giving us comfortable, untroubled sailing with time to look about and savour the river under a glorious early summer sky.

Our first destination was Stangate Creek and then a quiet sail up into Lower Halstow Creek. The plan – to stop over outside the village dock and visit what was once a local pub. After mooring and a short row in the dinghy, we were soon ashore walking beside the freshwater stream that issues into the old brickworks dock. The welcoming Three Tuns public house provided sustenance and a glass of beer. Alcohol is 'strictly' limited during underway hours aboard *Whimbrel* – all my crews know this foible of mine: something I have never thrown off from my seafaring days! Incidentally, the dock has been home to the spritsail barge *Edith May* for most of the last two decades, but she was away.

Departing, a weaving course was taken in amongst the saltings. First, we crossed the old stray way that once linked Milfordhope Marsh Island to dry land when the tide was out. Entering the shallow 'Hope' creek my brother and I cast a look across to Callows Wharf, where a house barge is now berthed: it was our 'last home' aboard the spritsail barge *May Flower*.

"Right, a little treat…" I said, "now through the Shoregate gap…" something one, but not the other had done.

There is little in the way of markings currently, but it has been well marked in the past. I once sailed through with the mate, working round the bends as the mud flats covered. Short withies helped, here and there. But once the tide is up, one can 'just go for it' keeping the land to one side and the edge of another 'road' where tell-tale bladderwrack marks its approximate position.

Sailing across the run of Otterham creek, we took a route 'under' Nore Marsh Island. Here, there are scattered buoys to be followed by the helm, who was left to it, while my gaze roamed the wilderness around, savouring.

On the way, I'd chatted about some of the area's history which can be seen lurking in amongst these marshes, if you know where to look. Sometimes *Whimbrel* was all but brushing the cord grass, waving in the run of the tide, causing mirth, for our cousin hasn't quite got used to this shallow water stuff!

Clearing Nore Marsh, a course was set across the run of the River Medway into and through Hoo Middle and West creeks. It makes a pleasant diversion and is well buoyed for there is a busy yard with an adjacent sailing club.

A brother and cousin come sailing…

The 'inshore route', as I've long-termed it, is fun. It's a sailing pleasure and the heady saline scents that pervade lift the soul. Fortunately, both shared my enthusiasm too. Secretly, I wondered if these joys for me were short, I dearly wanted them to continue for many years more, God willing.

Our last day was mundane in the extreme with a beat down river and reach and run for home. The mundane, had one spot of hilarity: one of the crew who had enjoyed a sail in little *Twitch* the previous evening, had forgotten (and I'd not checked!) to re-fit the centre plate cover. It resulted in a partially flooded dinghy, as it frolicked behind us, shooting sprays of water inboard every now and then. It was interesting to witness, but it gave us all a laugh. It reminded me of an occasion when I left the cover out on a run over from Smallgains Creek to Queenborough – the dinghy nearly sank!

We'd departed early, so with plenty of time on our side we anchored along Blackstakes for a ginormous brunch. This was after a lapse of my concentration, resulting in grounding on the shallow mud edge and our sticking fast! The tender's centreplate cover was obviously dealt with too, as well as bailing her out.

Thanks guys. You were a much-needed sanity tonic during a period of low morale.

Moving on, the mate and I had another weekend away on the boat too. We walked our lovely countryside and I continued to finish the annual maintenance – well continue it: it is in effect never finished on a wooden vessel!

As directed, I pitched up for my bone scan. Once inside the clinic, I joked with the male clinician, as he injected this 'solid feeling' liquid into my left arm, which later came out in a massive bruise, changing colour for many days. He didn't seem to have a sense of humour: he said, with a serious face, 'You do understand why you are here, don't you?'

Oooooooooops…I thought, as I nodded, for it felt as if I was being severely reprimanded. I decided to stay quiet, not uttering anything further. Kill-joy!

Then some explaining about heights etc and I was being slipped inside the scanning machine, a tunnel, which came close to my nose giving a feeling of claustrophobia. And that was that.

The first bit of good news followed: the scan results came back negative…

I wrote a blog on my website telling men (and women for it is women who mainly press their men to go to a doctor) about my experience, giving a warning to all. People contacted me in numbers, some from afar but most from closer to home. All said 'thank you' for the alert. Some had their own stories to tell. One, in particular, was a sailor from Washington State, United States of America, who 'ditch-crawled' among the rocky 'creeks' up into the Canadian Province of British Columbia. He'd had prostate cancer some ten years before and was open with aspects of treatment and afterlife. What was most comforting was the number of men who simply said, "I'll get tested…" In some cases, they have been very thankful indeed: they themselves were suffering without knowledge or intimation.

Later, a yachting magazine columnist picked up on all of this. He set to and wrote about a chap who had become locally known as the 'Prostate Prophet' and gave out 'a sailor's warning…' promising to have a test himself. I have continued down that vein: sailors and landsmen alike, it makes no difference. It is a killer and men need to take it on board.

The main trouble is men. Men just do not talk about health matters. Women do. They'll sit, sipping tea or coffee and discuss anything and if you believe the tabloids and women's natter mags, even down to the sexual performance of their men, so fear not, nothing is sacrosanct guys!

One bright day was an appointment to meet our son outside his London office – a boys evening. A quick march across London Bridge to the George public house for a glass or two of beer first. Then we hopped on a tube to the Oval Cricket Ground for an evening 20-20 cricket match. It is something that has become an annual event, starting some seasons earlier.

My string of hospital appointments, all on one day, arrived. Reaching the waiting room, my worry was initially squashed for I was flabbergasted by the number of men among those there – oncology covers a host of cancer problems. What I didn't realise then was that I was to bump into many the same chaps many times, over the next two years.

Christobel quietly read with occasional glances of reassurance. I tried to read the book brought along for 'another wait' but it was to no avail. I shut it and just gazed numbly round and into myself, I suppose.

The call came, late, but that was becoming 'normal'. First up was my visit to the specialist nurse – these are the nurses who have done additional training in aspects of ailment/treatments. I was ushered into an empty clinic room and we were sat down.

The door opened and a slim, confident-looking middle-aged lady stepped in. Smiling broadly, she turned and as we stood, shook our hands to introduce herself. She had 'that reassuring look…' but it didn't assuage the battering beating pulsing within my heart or the thoughts whirling and whizzing round my head.

"Right," the nurse said, sitting us down after pulling our chairs closer where we could see her computer screen, "we have a lot to go through…" I grimaced.

The first bit was a bit like 'engineering' as she sketched out a man's various procreative parts round the prostate. She described what did what and what happens when engaged in the sexual act. And what happens when a man wants to pass water. About valves, nerves, blood vessels, erections, etc, etc…

The next question came as a surprise, but I was fast becoming less phased by such things. She said, "How often do you have sex?"

"Well," I said, stalling a little, feeling somewhat abashed whilst trying to maintain eye contact. I blushed deeply too.

"We're an active married couple," my mate chipped in quickly as her hand left my knee where it had been resting. Opening her fingers out one by one, she added, "Over a week…we enjoy each other this much, usually…"

"Good…right…we'll talk about that…"

My cheeks were severely inflamed as I looked at the nurse and sheepishly nodded. I then watched inquisitively as she made a few notes.

The conversation and filling in of details on form after form and on the screen went on for quite some time. I was given a run through the level of cancer diagnosed and what that meant. It wasn't good but would have been far, far worse had I not asked for that test back in the winter. It was early summer by this point. And, as I was soon to learn, I was six months into my 'two years…maybe a bit more… if not spotted'.

We spent quite a period going through prostate removal, known as prostatectomy; something I had read about – brachytherapy; hormone treatment and radiotherapy. By this time, I was becoming fogged. I was also beginning to feel detached from any form of reality. Perhaps, inside, I was in denial still, as I had been since the first prostate test several months back. I well remember saying to someone in our circle, "Doctor said it wasn't a problem, so…"

"Now," she said, "depending on the treatment path you choose there will be an effect on your capabilities, but…" I shivered, thinking of the earlier question, but any further thoughts were stalled as she quickly continued, "there are things you can do…there are special pumps…rubber bands…I won't explain now…" Then, looking at Christobel, she added, "you may have to learn of new ways to…" I sensed an unspoken conversation going on, over my head, between women.

I'd been thinking of 'perhaps…the little blue pill'.

All through, my mate had been holding one of my hands or gripping my thigh, inflicting pain at times. I looked at her and could see her thoughts were tracking along with my own. I was in an utterly panicked mode by this point.

"What are your hobbies?" was another question. We both ran through the way we 'ran' our lives. "Sailing should be alright… but you might find walking long distances tiring or not possible, in time…"

Eventually, we were shown out to another waiting area. Both feeling somewhat speechless.

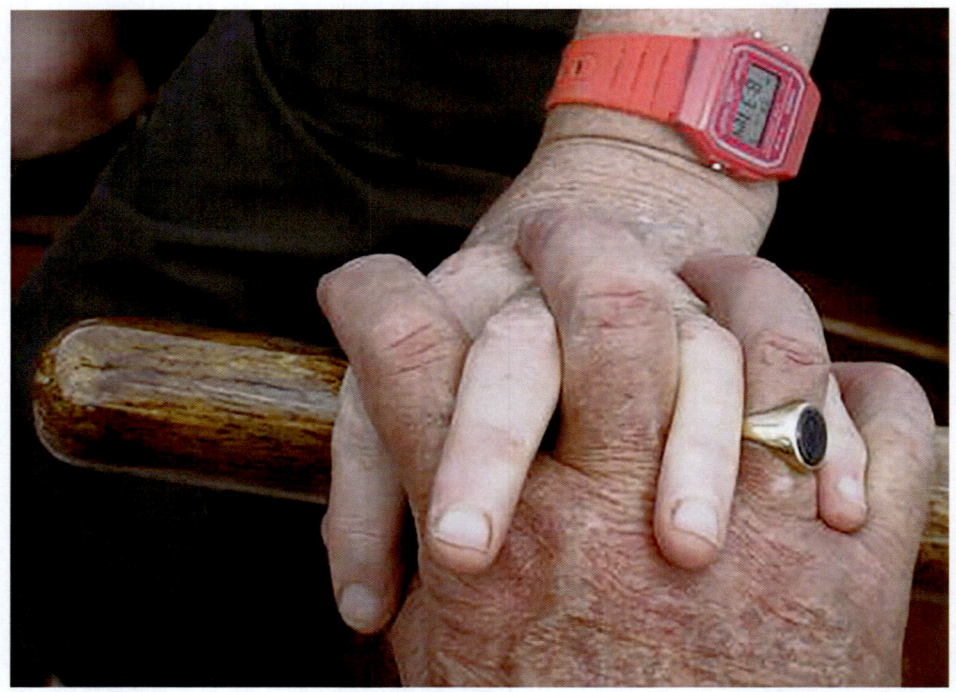

Togetherness…

Next up was the Oncologist. Before that though, there were pee flow tests to perform. No problems there, I was told!

Then an assistant came and said that the oncologist was running late and that his registrar would talk to us first, then the surgeon and finally finishing back with the oncologist himself…"I understand…" I said, trying to smile.

We were very shortly shown into a consulting room. In a corner opposite a window, a computer was whirring away, as they do. Upon its screen were gory-looking pictures of a view inside a body – my body it soon turned out. Then the registrar wafted in. Now and this isn't being in any way sexist: she was a vision indeed. Looking at me, I saw my mate's eyebrows lifting, up and down, as she grinned!

The registrar introduced herself, apologised for the specialist being held up. Then she swung onto her chair and crossed her legs. Sitting directly opposite, I was aghast to see her button fronted frock falling in sail-like folds, all awry. As she began to talk, all I could see were her long-tanned thighs climbing before me…I later wondered if this was all part of the way she worked: she was utterly unperturbed!

Boy, she was great though. She explained everything – including pointedly, again, asking us both about our marital life, how regular, etc…saying, "We can help protect that. She added, "If you have the injections (of female hormones) it'll be like clinical castration…but we can use a steady tablet treatment…"

Hell…I thought.

Then, it was the turn of the Surgeon to apply his magic. On his desk was a cutaway model of a man's lower body with removable bits. At times, the surgeon 'played' with a walnut-sized piece representing a prostate. All the time, another svelte female registrar draped herself against the door post next to the desk, adding a few words here and there. He, they, did an 'examination' for which Christobel was shuttered off by curtains.

It was explained to me that the cancer was all over one-half of the prostate and had begun to migrate out. One-half of the nerve system needed by a man to be able to perform was infected and would have to go. "We don't know what the other side really looks like until we can get at it…" he said, adding, "we would do a quick test on the table for cancer cells…if clear, reattach them." I looked at him, finally realising my facts of life. He went on to explain a removal would be done at a different hospital by a robot, driven by his hands. "If we can save the nerves we will," he concluded, smiling, with what I was becoming used to as a reassurance…

It would be my choice which route I went, I was told. Even for a removal – prostatectomy – I was advised that a period of radiation treatment would be necessary to mop up any lingering cancer cells in the surrounding tissue.

So, back to the oncologist – a genuinely nice man indeed. He was eventually 'the man' I was with throughout the journey that followed.

As we got up to leave, the oncologist looked up from making a note, said, "You know," he paused as if to let the next part sink in and added, "you'll not die from this…"

It was the second specialist who had now told me this. He added too, "We can fix it…so don't worry…" He smiled, in a reassuring way, as he got up to shake my hand and Christobel's as well.

A day or so after, I went for a sail, alone, on the tide. My mate was visiting some friends. I think we both needed a break from close company. Within *Whimbrel's* log there is a note for that day, it says: 'Saw specialist surgeon, oncologist and nurse – Not so good. T3a Gleason 8/9 cancer, vigorous and unpredictable. Remove or hormone/brachio/radiotherapy. Hmmm.'

When our plans changed so dramatically, we sat down and looked at our diary of important dates – largely all revolving round my hospital visits. Following the tri-appointment, it was down to me to come to a decision within no more than a few weeks as to which course of treatment I wanted to take. So, I bagged a long weekend away to take in the annual Thames Barge Match, which took place from Gravesend, a little way upstream of our 'home' in Sea Reach.

We sailed away on a Thursday, bound for Sharfleet Creek, off Stangate, itself off the River Medway. We anchored in one of our favoured spots along a mud edge abreast of the old military jetty once used by an army engineers garrison based on Burntwick Island.

The following day we enjoyed a delightful sail out of the river and up the Thames to Gravesend with a useful east south-easterly easing the way. Off Lower Hope though, it became more southerly, but with the tide in our favour it wasn't a hardship, with barely a couple of tacks needed…Various barges could be seen approaching from astern and one or two had been ahead of us for some while. I was looking forward to seeing barges off Gravesend: it was something I hadn't seen since my childhood when a participant as a child aboard our floating home, way back in 1962 and 1963.

But, importantly, it was on the way up the river that I came to my decision. I'd been on the helm and with the ease in which the passage was passing, had time to sort through my mind. I do believe though that it had already been made. We'd discussed it at length, agreeing to let it rest awhile. The mate had just brought some beverages up from below. Taking mine from her, I said, determinedly, "I've decided…"

"Right…"

"Medical route," I said. There were copious tears and kisses and a huge surge of relief. More recently, passing down that reach, along the Mucking Flats, the memory of that decision was clearly brought back to both of us.

As then, concentration is needed as the Ovens buoy falls astern and an eastwards course is made, for the Tilbury half-tide submerged tide 'deflectors' need to be cleared, so our 'celebrations' were short-lived until after we had moored!

Approaching the Ovens Buoy on way to Gravesend.

Upon mooring and 'freeing' myself from my mate, I got straight onto the phone and called my dedicated specialist nurse who was my point of contact. Having told her of my (our) decision, she said,

"Good, where are you?"

"Off Gravesend," I said, "away sailing..." adding, "be back on Monday morning."

She chuckled, then said, "Your prescription will be at the pharmacy waiting for you..." She added her congratulations too and wished us well. A few days later, upon arriving back at our moorings and tidying up, we drove directly to the hospital and there it was, all bagged, three months' supply.

We didn't see much of the barge match for the start was down near Cliffe Creek, essentially out of sight – something I was completely unaware of! There was very little wind and it had been a struggle for the engineless barges to get proper way on with the outgoing tide. Shame really.

We had a lazy day. In good conditions, it is lovely sitting off the shore at Gravesend as there is so much to see. The river can be a busy place, its fascinations enthralled me. A pleasant chap rowed over from a mooring, a member of the Thurrock Yacht Club. He ranged alongside for a natter – a fan, it soon turned out! I invited him aboard, but he just wanted to talk. It was gratifying, but I'm not sure about such adulation! I did get a bit of maintenance done, as usual. We both read. I watched the world go by, feeling strangely at peace...

Finally, barges began to reappear, bending to a welcome southerly breeze, providing a bit of a late afternoon colour and spectacle upon the busy river. I even remember what we had for supper – kebabs made with prepared marinaded cuts from a supermarket. They were lovely with a salad, washed down with a glass or two.

Ah, yes, the next morning, with a purposeful north-north-westerly we enjoyed a glorious sail down to the Nore and then into River Medway. We 'raced' the spritsail barges *Marjorie* and the *Niagara*, in that order, down Sea Reach. The *Marjorie* majestically swept past us off to port in a little more water over the Grain Flats. "Cor," I said, "her chine must be kissing the bottom..." Once inside the Medway, the *Niagara* began to overhaul *Marjorie* with her amazing windward ability. It was a joy to watch as we peeled off towards Queenborough in the West Swale.

Our summer plan had always been, to sail up to London, stopping at a few places on the way. Limehouse Marina was the planned stop-over harbour with a week provisionally booked, two months earlier. As my hospital appointments were now over for some considerable period until the following spring, we were free. So, with a lighter heart than I'd had for ages, I emailed the harbour office confirming our arrival date and time. We went off full of elation, having a fabulous time of it too.

At the end of our sailing summer, my elder brother who had come over from Canada came to stay. He had eight days 'for us' – all pre-planned in the deepest of Newfoundland winters. In a rather rapid conference, our younger sister who had missed out on her sail with her friends jumped at the offer of a five-day sail (written about elsewhere). It was a pity, we all thought, that our youngest sibling could be with us too!

There followed the many months on the medication, watching for any untoward changes. The hormone treatment acts as a closed-door to testosterone feeding the prostate cancer cells. An additional medication was given alongside, to nullify attempts of the hormone tablet to change my sex (grow breast tissue)! My chest and body hair soon began to 'disappear' at about the same time as 'we' both noticed a libido change. That was a sign for my mate to be the number one 'initiator'…a part of what the specialist nurse had talked about. Sorry if such words bother any readers, but it must be spoken about, for the sake of all men and yachtsmen. Any shyness I felt, had long before fallen overboard!

Another sign was a growing feeling of tiredness, a loss of energy and an inability to get on with things at a level previously enjoyed. This was frustrating. Part of that problem 'stayed put' beyond the ending of medication, two years down the line. Onwards, I think age may also be catching up…

I went into the next year, 2019, with a looming series of hospital visits. At some point, I had a visit to the hospital for my treatment control 'dots' to be marked. These are essentially three tattooed dots, which are likely to stay with me until my last day! Next on the list was a pre-med, then the brachytherapy, which was delayed a month. The delay wasn't for long, but I remember feeling an unprecedented level of stress at the time. The follow-up radiation sessions were clearly delayed too, obviously. A 'group' session preceded my radiation on what to expect, but I should have been called to an earlier session for it covered the brachytherapy element I'd already had. Wonderful!

Early in the year, I found myself afloat on a gloriously sunlit winter day enjoying a spanking sail. It was on the day before the birthday of the eldest of my two brothers. I posted a short film on a social media site, especially in his honour…

Valentine's Day walk, our picnic lunch…

I remember our walking a lot: the fresh air and countryside were additional tonics alongside my ability to keep on sailing. One walk comes to mind for it was on Valentine's Day. It was around 12 km taking in scenic climbs above the River Crouch and 'home' to the car, back along the river's wall. We stopped for our lunch break near where two old spritsail barges were hulked many years ago. Unpacking the lunch bits from my mate's haversack (she carries, I navigate…), I came across a little box of heart-shaped chocolates that she had slipped in when packing. Ah, it was such a sweet and romantic thought of hers. It made the day special.

When people talked to me, I tended to trivialise my cancer, treating it as if I had a simple common cold. My good mate would scold me and say, 'Don't be silly,' but I cannot remember feeling unwell throughout the period. Much of it has become part of my history, other bits seem as fresh as the day concerned.

As my Brachytherapy operation approached, I had the pre-med visit to the hospital which I thought was a complete waste of time: the self-same questions and samples were taken again a few days later – but who am I to wonder upon this procedure!

I went in for the brachytherapy operation feeling rather scared. It entailed an overnight stay in hospital. For me, it involved the insertion of 21 special hollow needles which penetrated through the soft patch in the underneath area, into the prostate. This was done under anaesthetic (look it up chaps – it wasn't so bad…). Upon coming to, I was wheeled into a special room where the needles were coupled up to an 'atomic' machine which, after the radiation nurse left and closed the door, radioactive material was fired into the prostate in a controlled dose set by the treatment procedure devised by the oncology team. It felt like someone was inside me, tapping out a message in a kind of morse code.

That was the easy bit. Those 21 needles were then removed without further anaesthetics by the oncologist himself…the nurses were so lovely, one, gently holding my hand and talking as another administered a little gas to alleviate the severe 'burning' sensations!

Not for the first time, I had a far, far, different experience on the ward, where I was tucked into a corner with all the ward's cleaning equipment. A salubrious spot to while away the hours. I had previously been told my catheter would be quickly removed, as leaving in longer than necessary caused damage. It stayed in.

Next morning the Surgeon came in to see how things were, noticing the catheter, he went 'ballistic' calling a nurse to fetch gloves! The nurse made motions to deal but was shooed away. "I can do it…" he said, sharply. He removed it with gentle ease, passing all for disposal.

It was later when being granted permission to walk to a toilet, a wad of padding applied to my 'wound' fell to the floor. I didn't even know it was there. It hadn't been checked, but surely…I just wanted to go home. Eventually, after several delays, I escaped!

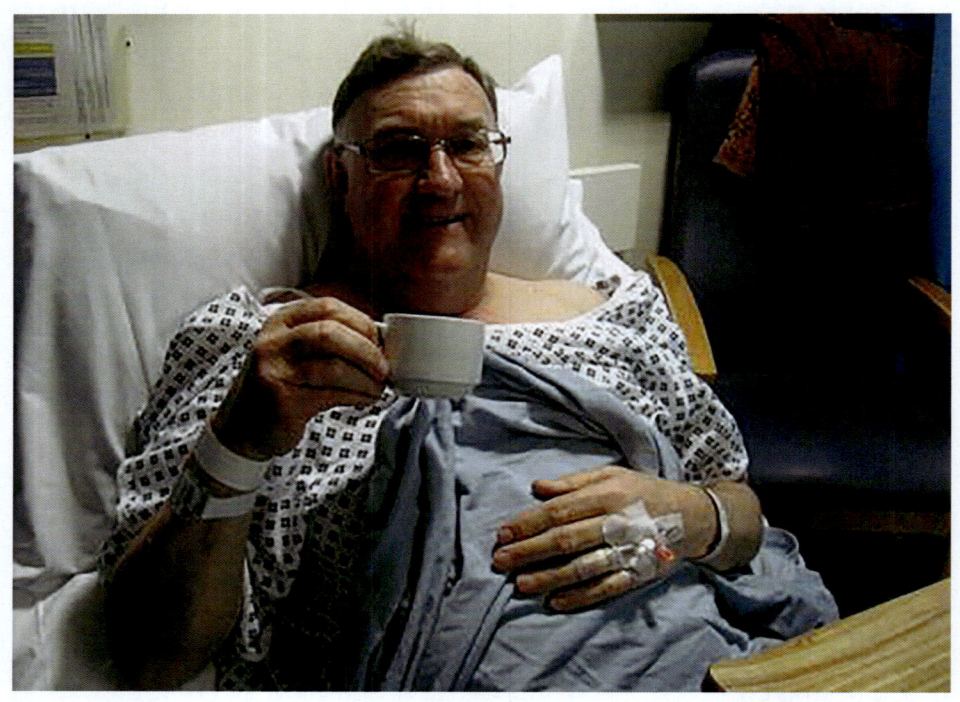

Post brachytherapy cuppa.

Then, I virtually went straight into my radiotherapy sessions, with a weekend in between. The staff was so lovely in this unit too, so caring, so friendly, so professional. Nothing seemed to be any trouble. It made the whole experience so much easier to handle. Before my first blast, I asked the staff to take pictures for a blog I was writing. I then had to tell all, about my sailing life, etc. One of them said, "That's a brave thing to do."

"No," I said, "men must be made aware…"

When on 'the slab' the 'affectionate' name I gave the bed of the radiation machine, the most important thing that one must remember and I was told this quite forcibly, "…stay absolutely still, do not move even for an itch…"

"Right," I said, grinning, "I'll do my best!"

So, I assumed, looking up at a lit picture set into the ceiling panels, this must be up there to help take one's mind off events. The powers to be at 'my' hospital had a picture of a view looking up through trees into a blue sky. Now, me being me, I suggested a beautiful sailing scene as an alternative. It wasn't taken up.

Christobel, the good mate she is, came up with an excellent wheeze for the end of each week's sessions. We took to dropping down to a local waterfront public house for a beer. Well, I drank the beer and she had coffee. A good deal, for sure. On one of these occasions, we met a sailing friend and ended up having 'another' well I think it was two. Strangely, I was a little sleepy that evening, but it was good to talk sense to another person outside my small family circle. Thanks, D.

The sessions were drawn out a little due to the calendar dates for Easter and a bank holiday that closely followed. During all that time, the weather was improving as the spring progressed, so I was able to get maintenance done on *Whimbrel*. This, due to my loss of energy levels, was done in chunks, but not only that, life very much revolved round the daily treatment regime. On a string of beautiful sunny days over the Easter period we jointly sanded *Whimbrel's* cabin sides and as preparatory work had also been completed, so the fresh varnish was applied too. Job done!

Over the bank holiday weekend, I was free of appointments for several days. "Can we go sailing…" I asked, wistfully. My mate had already got it planned!

We got away for a couple of nights with a trip on the River Medway. At the stage of treatment, I was at, it was a wonderful tonic to sail upon waters I have loved all my life, to feel the thrum of the boat's tiller. The scenes, the scents from freshly the fresh growth of plant life in the salt marshes. The bird life. Other boats and the fraternity of a Queenborough pub. I felt renewed and refreshed for the last couple of weeks of treatment.

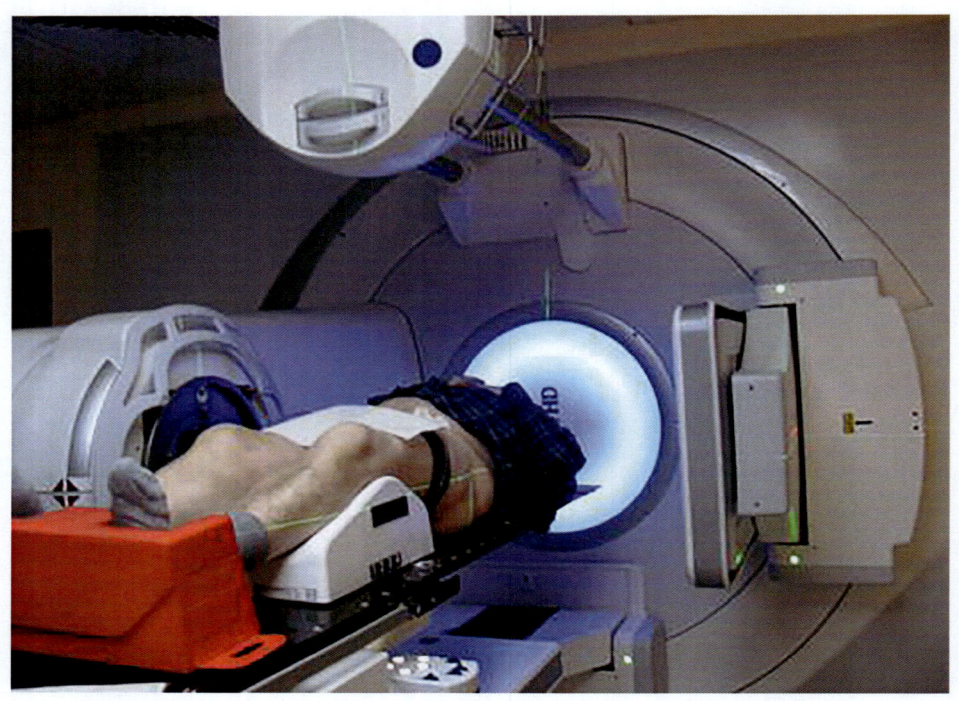

On the 'slab' as I affectionately termed it!

The final day soon came along. The weather was sublime. The wind forecast was good. The tide times suited. So, I said, "I'm off I for a morning sail later…" First though, that morning, a pair of blue tits which were nesting in a garden box had the first of many hatchings. We watched, enthralled, as we enjoyed our breakfast. It was a good sign.

So, departing from my creek on the eastern tip of Canvey Island, I sailed across towards the Westcliff shore, then along towards Leigh-on-Sea before heading back out towards my home creek. Flocks of Brent geese were out there still, awaiting the right conditions to set off on their long flights north to the Russian tundra bordering the arctic sea. The boat frolicked in the conditions. As the bow 'scrunched' the small waves. Occasional showers were thrown up and I was entranced as they sparkled diamond-like in the brightness. It was a magically good sail on a good day. Heck, it was fantastic.

I arrived for my last session, triumphant and radiating happiness. Entering the waiting room, I was escorted straight in – early! The radiologist, the senior on duty as far as I could tell, put her arm round me, gave me a hug and said, "Congratulations, last session today…" as I handed over a card and a box of handmade chocolates for them all. The bonhomie carried through to the treatment room and once up on the 'slab' one of the two operators said, "What have you been up to this morning?"

"Got out for a glorious sail," I replied, grinning broadly. "Ah, it was wonderful." I laughed as I laid back, thinking of something… One of the operators looked at me and smiled. Then, still grinning I added, "I'm sailing through life…"

"I hope you do," he said. Both of us laughed, heartedly.

The two operators finished positioning the treatment table heights, checking and rechecking them. Then, they were done. One said, "Good luck…" and both departed. The red light came on and I steadied myself to receive my last dose of radiation. In a mere moment of reflection, as a calm came over me, I thought, *yes, you have been sailing through life, joking aside…*

As I lay there, all sorts of thoughts ran through my mind. The 'What if's' had I not demanded to have the prostate test those 16 months earlier. The warning I'd been given that had I not, then within two years onward, no more, I'd be staring down the barrel of oblivion. The love and support of family, friends and complete strangers. My sister, trekking 25 km along 'The Ridgeway' in support of a prostate cancer charity and the wide support she had. My thankfulness for my treatment and for all of those who had cared for me.

Before I left the theatre, I had hugs and words of good wishes from the staff present. All wanted me to ring the 'finished treatment bell' which hung in the main reception area. Christobel said, "Oh no!" And I did, to some applause from people awaiting their own appointments.

All along, I had taken others with me: many men had taken up the challenge to my call 'Get Tested – Stay Alive' and they too were into their own treatment journeys. One, a friend and mooring neighbour, had initially been hesitant. Sadly, he had a similar level problem, but was thankfully, at the time, being treated. We follow one another's test results a bit like checking a pool's coupon.

So, with all hospital treatment over apart from the initial three-monthly PSA blood checks and a few minutes with the oncologist, I was free for the summer. It meant my regular crews could come sailing again. For some it was an annual treat, greatly looked forward to. It also meant freedom for the mate and me. It meant too that I was able to fulfil a promise made to a New Zealander – a coastal sail into the River Alde. A tale written about in this collection.

Christobel applying Whimbrel's antifouling…

It wasn't all plain sailing though. Sometime towards the close of my 'radiation year' and two-thirds of the way through my hormone medication, I detected a hardening of the male breast tissue, with it some soreness. I was developing odd lumps on either side and I thought, *heck, my sex is changing…*I told my astonished mate…

An appointment at my surgery soon had me beating a path to the local hospital breast clinic within no more than a few days. Arriving, I was told to change into a gown but keep lower clothing on. The gown was a fetching pink-like hue. I was sat among a group of women, feeling rather self-conscious and foolish.

I was called. Heads looked up, I blushed deeply. Christobel

said, "It's alright…don't worry…" as she trotted beside me. I had the works. Questions galore, what medication, a gentle feel, inked circles drawn on my chest, then back out to waiting room. Another call – down to the mammogram room! Now women will know all about these…yes, it bloody hurt and there wasn't much for the lovely radiographer to get hold of either, to squeeze between a pair of plates! After that, back to the waiting room. A further call – an ultra-scan. While the lady doctor was doing this, she said, "Have you lost a lot of body hair?"

"Yes," I said, adding, "especially on the chest and downwards," pointing. There were two women in the room, and they looked at one another, knowingly. Little else was said.

As I was dismissed, I passed an 'off the cuff' remark about inadvertently changing sex…a few paces down the alleyway, I heard a peel of outright laughter. I smiled. Clearly, I'd made somebody's day at least!

Finally, I was ushered back to the specialist. "Don't worry," he said, "you have a touch of Gynecomastia…" and handed me a leaflet. He explained that it was a phenomenon that affected many older men and sometimes 'chubby' adolescent boys, "but," he continued, "it should disperse as the effects of the medication reduce in your body, but it'll take some time…"

That was it. The disquiet I felt was only marginally squashed. The lumps have remained.

It was exactly two years after that glorious sail up the Thames to Gravesend to witness a barge match that I was taken of all medications. It was a good day. The first journey was over. But I know that the longer journey is now in progress: nothing is certain in life. You can keep fit in mind and body, eat sensibly and hope. That is all.

Well, then we hit the 2020 Corona Crisis with a pandemic of Covid-19 sweeping the globe. At the time I was due for a prostate blood test, the whole of the United Kingdom went into a national lockdown. The world and the way we humans operated, ground to a shuddering halt!

My prostate tests have continued to be 'very positive indeed…' the oncologist said, a year after my radiation treatment. "Virtually zero…" he told me.

The specialist has always asked the same questions and at a further check, Christobel was sitting close by me while I was talking during a phone appointment – instituted at the start of the Covid pandemic. Upon hearing the awaited question, Christobel chortled and quickly called out "No problem there…" Yes, it was the erection one!

The first time he asked this question, he said 'election' by mistake – it was just after a general election. "Pardon…" I asked, looking at him. The oncologist laughed, correcting himself. I blushed, saying quickly, "We're okay…"

Still chuckling, he said, "Good. Check again in six months." On the other chair, my wife was grinning wickedly.

Peace and serenity after a late afternoon sail.
Yes, without doubt life is precious.

During the autumn of 2021, a test letter arrived, and I booked a blood test in readiness for an early January follow-up telephone consultation. Around Christmas the appointment was cancelled. I shuddered. It was due to Covid delayed catch-up work. The new date was several months onward, so I followed up the blood test for it was due. As I write, the appointment approaches during the week of our wedding anniversary. Although, not feeling unhappy, it would be a huge weight of my mind when I hear all continues to remain, 'very positive…'

Many people, me included, went through a period of intense introspection during the first lockdown. Life and what is held dear. What is of importance and what really matters became conscious and subconscious thoughts in moments of quiet reflection. There were many opportunities whilst taking 'the daily exercise' for those thoughts to be analysed. My mate and I discussed much together too, on those walks. Many of the tales found in this volume will have a connection with my treatment period and the Covid Crisis, until the latter, itself, became all-consuming and 'controlled' our daily lives.

One thing we agreed on utterly: there were so many other people in a far, far worse situation. In fact, we considered ourselves as part of a largely 'protected' group and felt damned lucky indeed…

2
Twitch Gets a Ducking!

"Come on," I said, "let's have a spin round the Wade."

The boat had just picked up from the beach where we'd put *Whimbrel* aground to scrub her bottom on the northern end of Stone Point – inside that sheltered patch that appears as the tide drops away.

The wind, what there was of it, was a light westerly and we cleared out of the 'hole' and out past Island Point under sail. We set to, tacking up Hamford Water with the flood tide under us, giving a good lift. Our scrubbing shorts and shirts were flapping gently from the guard rails to dry a little for they would go into a washing machine later, but never mind that, I had a mug of tea and more in the cosied pot, close by.

"Fancy a bit of cake too..." I said, looking pleadingly at my mate. She pursed her lips and dropped below to oblige me. As it was handed out, smiling, I murmured, "Thank you darling..."

Twitch, our lug-sail dinghy, 'trotted' happily along behind us, alternately tugging and surging a little on her painter whilst skipping through the small wavelets in the tide's run. We passed through a menagerie of anchored yachts in the area below Kirby Creek. Few craft anchored above 'Kirby' due to the shallowness of that open expanse. Looking up Oakley Creek, we saw seals cavorting, before slipping beneath the water in their effortless way to scoop up another meal.

The mate was helming. "Okay," I said, "begin your turn into Kirby...boat will slip across the tide..." We were soon into the entrance, well clear of the spit running out from Skipper's Island. The creek was once a busy anchorage, but for some years there have been shellfish beds within, with warning of consequences if you anchor and damage produce. But, up towards the head of the creek there are a few private moorings.

Scrubbed bottoms!

At a patch of saltmarsh forming Honey Island, locally known as 'Honeypot', the channel splits. One channel turns west of the island to eventually dissipate amongst a tangle of cord grass and purslane under the south side of Skipper's Island. The remains of an old barge, I'd visited lay in there too. Our course lay to the east of 'Honeypot' to pass 'north' of a further mass of saltings which has formed an island of some magnitude, growing, year by year. I chuckled.

"What now?" asked my mate whilst continuing to look at the birdlife fluttering round us.

"Well…you know the story…"

"What? No, I don't. Come on."

"I went aground on that piece some seasons ago when sailing alone…" It had been much to my chagrin for it was witnessed by a trip boat and her passengers!

My mate laughed whilst poking my ribs and said, "You got off…" but she surely wanted to say, "serves you right…"

Approaching the first of the islands, we exchanged waves with a family group aboard their yacht, but I concentrated more on our route, with a turn 'eastwards' close by a landing onto Horsey Island – the very spot where the fictional children in Arthur Ransome's famous book, *Secret Water* had their camp. The island is a private place and landing is not generally permitted.

We continued to happily sail along. The wind came onto the starboard quarter as we passed down the northern side of the second marshy island, on a generally south-easterly course. We were then deeply within the mere, or more correctly, The Wade. Abreast of a point of saltings hanging tongue-like off the underside of Horsey Island the channel divides, narrowing considerably within each. Up the western side of the tongue, there is a creek used by the island's boat. I saw it, in the distance, drawn up on what looked from my vantage, a rough sort of slip.

Of the two channels, one runs off south to twist eventually into Kirby Dock where spritsail barges once operated to and from a mill. The old mill is now converted into a desirable residence. There is supposed to be a public landing, but the marsh has claimed it. A private landing exists with signs warning one away…The channel we wanted ran pretty much east, before supposedly turning south, then east again, a little south of the middle of the expanse. The trip boat, having done a short excursion into Hamford Water, probably, was some distance astern.

The picture on our GPS map's screen seemed to correspond to a satellite picture I had and I confidently sailed on. The Twizzle, the creek running into the mere from the east at the foot of the Walton Channel wasn't so far away. Neither was the marina with its massed array of silvery masts glistening in the light. I made a southward turn, the wind full on the beam. Boom well slacked off to port. I was beginning to think that we should have taken the main down for this shallow water slalom, but…

In a gust, *Whimbrel* picked up speed. The light airs of earlier had grown into a decent sailing breeze. I had a feeling we were sailing too fast. I scanned ahead, swivelling my eyes, looking for any marks, spotting a buoy some way ahead, wondering if it was a passage marker.

Then, without warning, the boat felt light on the helm, slewing a little, as she felt the bottom. It all happened too quickly. I had no time to do anything other than push the helm over as her momentum drove her on. We were fast aground. Looking over the transom, the rudder had a hundred millimetres less water up its blade.

"Damnation!" I exclaimed, as my mate looked at me.

Twitch, the dinghy, initially ran up alongside to starboard, but while I was starting the engine and the mate was dropping the jib, the dinghy bobbed back round the stern to range along the port side.

Away across the water towards Horsey Island, the tripper boat was slipping along the saltings edge with her hoard of holidaying passengers. I could feel many eyes drilling into us, wondering what the heck we were playing at!

"The dinghy..." the mate called from forward, returning my concentration to matters more pressing. I turned my gaze towards *Twitch* and was horrified to see her heeling over for apparently no reason that I could see.

We weren't going anywhere, so I untied the painter and began to take it forward. It was then that I spotted the problem. The mast top of *Twitch* had become entangled in *Whimbrel's* mainsail reefing lines down the sail's leach. It was the little fluttery flag that was caught at its hoist.

I then 'dived' back aft to attempt to free the little burgee. It had no intention of coming free and, alas, nature's tidal forces rushing past us pulled the little boat over and she filled. Sinking beneath the surface I saw that things such as centre plate and her rudder were still lashed. Little of consequence would be lost. As the little boat filled her mast came free, as it also partially pulled out of the dinghy too. So, as the tide took full hold of the flooded dinghy, I watched, as the mast at its drunken angle, disappeared under the water!

"Bloody Heck..." I shouted. The mate looked at me. "Drop the anchor over," I called, with a heightening of passion, adding, "I'll get the main off..." I had to drag it down. With a couple of lines round the flapping sail, I turned my attention back to the dinghy.

The dinghy was lying on her side with the mast wedged under the curve of *Whimbrel's* bottom. Initially, I couldn't move her. Due to the depth of water, the dinghy's sunken side was clearly digging a furrow in the soft, muddy bottom as *Whimbrel* moved a little. Then, as the anchor bit and we swung to starboard a little, the dinghy began to free itself.

"A bit more chain," I called, panting from my effort to free *Twitch* from her immersion by heaving on the painter.

"I think the mast is digging in the mud…" I called. "Bit more chain…"

After what seemed an age, *Whimbrel* slid forward again and as her anchor snubbed, she swung her stern to starboard, freeing the dinghy's mast.

A tug on her painter and an awash *Twitch* came upright, wallowing in her flooded state. I grinned at the mate, as I gradually picked up the dinghy's bow and allowed water to flow out over her transom. Inside, was a mass of mud. The rolled-up sail was muddy too – that would wipe off. The mate quickly pulled out a couple of fenders. So, with *Whimbrel* now riding to her anchor, the muddied and soaked dinghy sat not so serenely alongside…

"Okay…" I said, "I'll climb over and bail the remainder out… pass the dip bucket, can you…" Climbing carefully aboard and kneeling on the centre thwart, I bailed the worst out, scooping most of the mud out too. Soon, a semblance of order and normality was restored.

We were a chastened crew aboard *Whimbrel* as we departed from our short, enforced, anchorage and backtracked a little to find the 'deep' water. I hadn't gone onwards for I'd seen a patch of 'grass' ahead of us earlier. The saga seemed to have gone on for hours, yet it was just a handful of minutes…

It was a twisting route we followed on the GPS and in no time the inner tail of the Twizzle was safely reached, where fenders and mooring lines were readied for a sedate and controlled arrival at Titchmarsh Marina.

The author enjoying an evening dinghy sail – after the event!

Upon mooring, whilst the mate went off to do the laundry, the dinghy was thoroughly cleaned out. At the top of the mast, a homemade turning block for the blue streamer usually to be seen fluttering was found to have broken during the earlier fracas.

The marina shop had just the bit with a spare in the packet and *Twitch's* blue streamer once again lifted, snaking in the breeze.

I forgot about the sail: the next time I hoisted it; I was forcibly reminded of my folly as a shower of mud dropped out over me!

How funny.

3
Silted and Lost?
Stour and the Wantsum Passage...

"The river's quiet today...only one ship coming up..." I murmured gazing out into Long Reach whilst making my way round the wooden walkway over the creek's muddy surface towards the boat's mooring. It was a surface pockmarked with scattered patches of limp cord grass. Too early for the new spring growth. Then I grinned, thinking of my mate's enjoyment of samphire – the posh name for glasswort. I saw the first signs of the annual crop poking provocatively from the mud where it had germinated during the recent neap tide cycle.

As I was about to make an abrupt turn away from the view, I looked seawards, further afield. Far off, I saw several vessels, hull down, away on the eastern horizon where there was a deep-water anchorage off the South Shoebury. And, far off in the Oaze Deep, a brownish trail drifted in the haze, indicating a ship below the horizon settling into sea-speed bound to far off to distant lands. I, however, hadn't time to stand and gaze. The tide was rising. I had a boat to get ready for sea and I'd not yet reached her.

Walking onwards my mind travelled back further, to another time. Ships were smaller in the early years of the last century so a far greater number were needed to shift the cargoes being carried – hence the belief that hardly any tonnage moved on the river. The Port of London was probably still the United Kingdom's largest multi-cargo port, excluding oil terminals such as Sullum Voe in the Shetland Isles. Gazing eastwards, another shape appeared many miles away in the Oaze channel. *Ah yes*...I thought, as I finally stepped aboard my clinker sloop, *it was a much busier place once...* Yes, but one modern container ship represented a fleet of ships of yesteryear! "Be more movement later though..." I said, aloud, my thoughts on sailing over to Kent.

Continuing my thoughts, my mind then traversed to far more distant times, back to the Roman Era. Shipping had then come from the English Channel 'through' Kent to The Swale, inside the Isle of

Sheppey. Coming round the Swale the route out into the Thames was through the Yantlet…"The inshore passage," I murmured, saying, "I'd love to do it too!"

The route began from the 'Downs' north of present-day Deal and into the River Stour at Rutupiae (Richborough), near Sandwich, where the Roman town is still laid out within its fortified walls on the edge of the River Stour. As the Stour threaded round the underside of Thanet, the route used the River Wantsum, northward, to an estuary near Reculver. It was a route well used by the Romans and surely other coastal traders of the time too. The Saxons sailed up the channel, landing on the soft underside of the Isle of Thanet. Today, the Wantsum was a mere drain. I chuckled, remembering a print I'd purchased. It was taken from Barclays Dictionary of 1851 and showed the Isle of Thanet with the River Wantsum open on the North Kent coast.

Bede, in the eighth century, I'd read, said that the channel was three furlongs wide, that is around six hundred metres, but even then, it was becoming a shallow meandering route through mudflats and marsh. A century later, the Vikings used the channel and the River Stour for their raid on Canterbury in 839. However, the channel's demise was ultimately manmade, for during the Norman period several centuries of land reclamation, inning, by Augustinian monks, further reduced the waterway. It became a mere drainage channel. During the fifteenth century, there was still a ferry, but by around 1550 the way onto Thanet was by a ford. The ford finally became a raised causeway at the 'waterside' village of Sarre.

"Less daydreaming…" I murmured, chiding myself for dilly-dallying, "boat won't get herself ready." So, I got on with honking the jib to the forestay and rolling up the mainsail cover. Finally, I hoisted the burgee and it fluttered in the generally north-westerly air. I was ready, just beating the tide. By the time I put the kettle on and prepared a mug for tea, the boat was showing signs of lifting. There were odd creaks sounding round me, then with an audible 'sigh' I heard the centre plate take up on its slackened lifting wire.

Leaving the kettle to come to the boil when it was ready, I started the engine and put the mooring lines 'ashore'. Looking up and down the creek I gave the engine a 'blast' and the boat slipped nicely out.

The wind was from the west. "Yep…sail out." I spun the boat and with the engine on idle, I hoisted the main, as we forged slowly up with the tide. The jib was quickly run up and I slipped back aft, leaving the halyards to tidy in a few minutes.

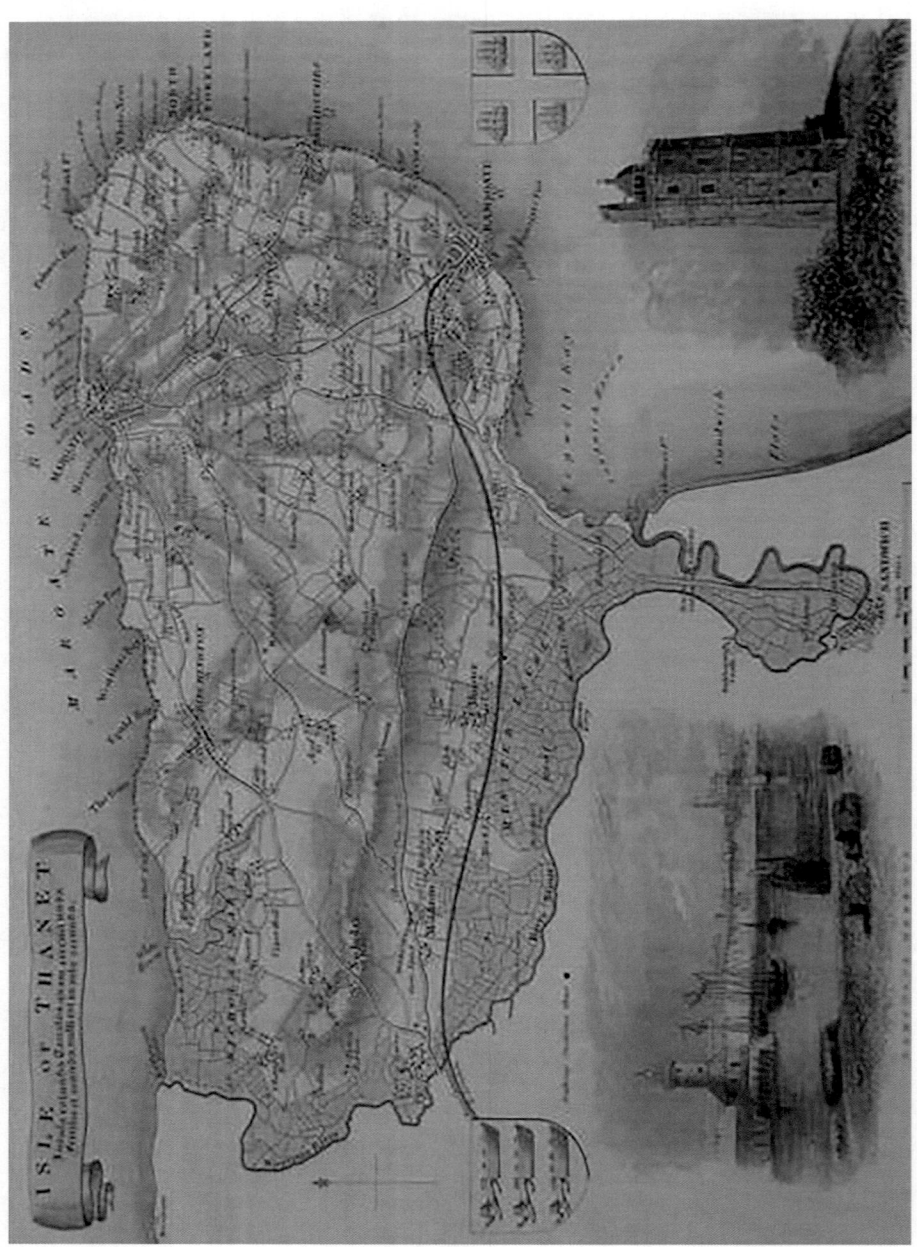

Route of Stour and Wantsum forming The Isle of Thanet – from Barclays Dictionary 1851. Author's collection.

Back on the tiller, I turned into a tack. As the breeze filled the backed jib, I let the mainsheet run out. With the bow all but pointing outwards, the jib sheet was released and we were on a run out over the tide. The idling engine was then shut down. At that point, the kettle made itself known with its vibrating roar of a whistle. I nipped below to fill my mug…

"That's better," I murmured, to no one other than myself and my 'mistress' who, I believe, was enjoying the moment too!

A chap was leaning on a walkway handrail, watching. I raised my mug. Drifting across the breeze, I heard, "Good day for it…" I grinned back at him. Whether or not he saw, I couldn't tell, but he raised an arm in farewell…

Yes, I thought, across to the Kent shore. It was something not done for a little while. Clearing the creek's entrance, I headed south, clearing a series of humped banks of shell and shingle. These are marked now but hadn't always been and I'd often seen boats head directly for them and coming to an abrupt halt!

Satisfied I was clear of the humps, I put a bit of east in our heading to account for cross tide effects to our course. As I settled, my thoughts travelled back to that old route again.

Yes, that inshore route had continued through the Swale and after turning north up past where the ship dock sits at Ridham and bridges just above, the channel probably ran through a long-closed route through what was now Chetney Marsh. I chuckled: the marsh still had remnants of a waterway within its walled boundary and the sea was precariously kept at bay against the rise of sea level and the southern land tip – sinkage back-lash caused by the last ice age. To my mind, there were two possible routes, but I am far from qualified to argue for this! What is true though is that it was a short jump from the Swale to Stangate Creek. During high tides boats nowadays seen across the marshes, seem to be sailing towards one another. It is an uncanny sight…

The passage had then either cut a dash through the Yantlet Channel, into the Thames, if London bound, or out of the Medway's mouth if a passage northward was needed. In that case, the inshore route was across the estuary and into the Havengore, which was then a wide and deep passage into the Roach and Crouch rivers, taking the Crouch's old route through what is now the Rays'n swatchway. The Crouch had a totally different run in those times too.

Meanwhile, I was sailing gamely across the tide towards the distant Yantlet Beacon. With some distance still to go, I was watching for the approach of outbound and inbound shipping too. Reaching the deep water of the Yantlet Channel, I crossed in a short time and once clear, relaxed again. The channel's name was probably an extension of the cut through the Isle of Grain, perhaps being given to a channel from one no longer in use.

For a short while, I watched the sun sparkling on the wavelets that nearly always exist in this reach of the Thames. Even on very quiet days, the water's surface is in motion from the turmoil from within its body as it ran into the Thames gulley. Those forces are churned into short sharp seas on a wild windy day. But on this day, it was a hypnotising experience. It was on such occasions that time could move on without notice. That was when things could go wrong!

So, breaking free, I began thinking ahead to where I was bound, I murmured, "Won't go in," to myself, of course and thought too, *yes, done it a few times*…Suddenly chuckling, I remembered a funny, "I touched the bottom once," I said, laughing. Yes, indeed. It was with another sailor aboard and I'd not kept us up to the bank of sand and shell that almost closes the Yantlet's entrance. You must sail close in along it and swing round the end into the creek, where there is a pool of sorts inside, remaining after the tide has gone…but, as said, not on this day!

I wrote in *Rochester to Richmond* about the gunnery test base that once operated from just inside the creek and a visit to the old dock. I wrote too about the closure of the creek with a dam at its southern end where it was named Colemouth Creek, off the River Medway, so I won't go into it again, other than lament at its loss.

I was by then closing the beacon, so, instead of continuing with my reminiscing, I took proper regard for our position. I decided to pass the beacon, come round onto the other tack, or reach and sail back over to the Essex shore to somewhere near Chalkwell, before heading into to my creek. I had plenty of time.

I was soon away again, remembering a stay in Faversham over an anniversary for a few nights. It was at the start of my 'prostate saga', but I was still firmly in the 'head buried' stage then. On one of the days, we drove towards Canterbury and paid our respects to Joseph Conrad who is buried in Canterbury Cemetery at Harbledown. From there we had gone on to Reculver to look at the old relic, but more importantly, to find the remains of the northern end of the River Wantsum.

The River Wantsum, from its juncture with the River Stour, weaves in a generally north-westerly direction across the wide heavily farmed flatlands. Those fields were once mud and salt marsh of course. On the way, it passes close to Sarre, the old ferry point and location of a ford which became a raised causeway called The Sarre Wall. The new road follows the old across the flatlands and runs straight into the village instead of following the old route round the old village quay. I walked down to the old road bridge and gazed upon the waterway, wondering.

Leaving Sarre, the old river passes beneath the modern Thanet Way, the A299, where the waterways course turns east, then after nearly a kilometre it kicks north, sharply and runs towards the coast, by which point it is nothing but a ditch. At the seawall, the 'river' bends in a banana fashion and flows west for a short length before petering out in a dry gulley near a shellfish farm inside the sea defences, directly below Reculver. Many years ago, the inimitable Charles Stock tried to get his little gaffer up the waterway. He made it for some distance, punting through reeds. It probably could be traversed by canoe, should one wish to have a go!

Sitting outside the sea wall at the point of the final westward turn, there is a small indent covered by scrub and salting above the beach. This was the river's 'last' estuary. Along the westerly run sits a sluice, relieving the land of any excess water, nearly two kilometres from Reculver. There are no east/west roads north of the Thanet Way, only farm tracks: it is a land very much under threat! The field systems seem to follow the waterway's last route with 'strips of field' on either side, reflecting the inning process.

Site of the lost Kent coastal village of Hampton.

When the river still ran with a reasonable flow out into the Thames estuary, some two hundred and fifty years ago, the natural drift was to the east. Along with that, there was a bank running westward towards Hearn Beacon (now Herne Bay), protecting the entrance to the west. On a 1727 map the bank, the Klippe Horse, extended offshore some distance and a series of sands swept broadly eastwards; the Last, the Spell, the Woolpack, the Spearn and Margate. Buoyed channels were shown between the Last and Spell sands and the Spell and Woolpack sands which had a channel of greater width.

H. Muir Evans in his interesting 1940 book, *A Short History of the Thames Estuary*, wrote about the Horse in the neighbourhood of Reculver being described in 1826 as being of small dimensions. It was clearly decreasing, for by 1892 an estuary chart I have, shows a sand bank named Reculver Sand off the shore with inshore route channels – Copperas and Horse – cutting through. The previous sands are by then 'shredded' and the Woolpack barely existed.

Today, the Woolpack has 'drifted' further offshore; the Copperas and Gore are channels, beneath the hooked shaped sand aptly called

Margate Hook. It should also be said, perhaps, that to the west the fishing village of Hampton disappeared into the sea. It was a fishing village with an oystery. Further developed during the 1870s, it was abandoned by 1916 and lost due to the forces of longshore drift erosion by the end of 1921, even though a rocky promontory thrusts from the coast here at the western side of modern Herne Bay. The remains of a disused stone pier juts from the shore.

"Ah yes…we went there," I murmured, "Hampton that is, before going on to Reculver…" We found a 'history board' telling of what happened and that was that.

The Reculver Towers on their Roman rampart.

At Reculver, we found the sheer size of the Roman fort's walls staggering for their size alone, never mind the quality of what is left – Regulbium, built during the third century, to guard the entrance to the River Wantsum. The two towers were interesting too. They are the remaining twin towers to St Mary the Virgin, Hillborough, Reculver. The church was demolished c1816 due to subsidence and a new one built inland and a little west. Trinity House stepped in and bought the towers in 1810 for their obvious facility as landmarks on the edge of a generally featureless estuary landscape. Groynes were built to protect the soft cliff fronts. Trinity House removed the spire-like tops to the towers and they remain useful to this day!

The Yantlet Beacon had long been left behind and the West Nore Sand was away to my starboard side, so I looked east and west, up and down the channel, searching for ship movements. Nothing, but a tug with a wall of frothy white water spewing from her bow was coming up the Nore or Jenkin Swatch, bound, I had no doubt, for the new container terminal upstream. The tug would leave poor *Whimbrel* dancing a polka when the wash hit her from astern, that was clear. "Better keep an eye…" I muttered: there was another occasion when a tug heading out to the Oaze produced a wash which climbed over the quarter onto the poop deck, splashing into the cockpit. Nasty!

The River Wantsum near Sarre.

Once the tug's wash had dissipated, I dropped below to put the kettle on and prepare a mug for some tea. There was no traffic to be concerned about and *Whimbrel*, on a reach, looks after herself nicely enough.

The kettle soon boiled and sipping my tea I began remembering more of the trips we'd made out 'Thanet way' – been several, I was sure. So, "Let's see," I said, 'I'll start at Pluck's Gutter, I think, just below Sarre…"

At Plucks Gutter, the Great Stour and Little Stour join to run, hand in hand, to the sea. Upstream of 'the gutter' was the Wantsum junction too, south of Sarre, where 'we' were earlier. It is a flat, rural landscape with humpback bridges carrying roads over the waterways. It is a 'wet land' and on a rainy day, when I was there, exceedingly wet, on river and land. I remember gazing briefly at some boats upon the water for they looked as bedraggled as I was soon feeling. My notes show the wetness of that day too, with smudged print and penned scribbles!

When the Roman's stopped off on their expeditionary visit a good number of years before the eventual 'invasion', the river system flowed into an estuary and a shallow sea. Ebbsfleet, on the Isle of Thanet, sat closest to the river and sea at the time, not being cut off until the thirteenth century. Concrete evidence of Roman occupation was found during the construction of a new road, the Richborough Way during the last decade. It was thought from Julius Caesar's own description of landing on 'an open shore' to be Pegwell Bay for they came down past high cliffs. Caesar came twice, in 55 BC and 54 BC, leaving after he concluded a treaty binding Britain to Rome…Saint Augustine landed here in AD 597, as did the Saxons in AD 449.

The walls of Rutupiae (Richbororough), near Sandwich.

On the mainland, close by, the Romans built a fortified town, a gateway to Britain. They named it Rutupiae, Richborough to us. It sat on the edge of high ground, which came down to the water in a protected part of the coast. The fort was a fascinating place to visit. Boy, the base of what was once the grand gateway was huge. A picture had me thinking of the Arc de Triomphe in Paris. A roadway ran down to the 'seaward' side which had long been lost. A rail line and the modern run of the River Stour cuts across where walls should be. They weren't desecrated: the sea ravaged what the Saxon's didn't. It was just the same as the fort at the entrance to the River Blackwater where St Peter's Chapel was built by Saint Cedd, the fort largely 'washed' into the sea.

Over time, as the area silted up from Pegwell Bay south of Ramsgate Harbour, down towards Deal, a new land was created. The river, needing a way, continued to the sea in a convoluted fashion from the underside of Thanet at Ebbsfleet. It turned south to the port town of Sandwich where it abruptly turned back north with loops here and there. Eventually, after the Port Richborough (a relatively new place) and Ebbsfleet, it reaches the sea in Pegwell Bay. There was a flood relief channel, the Stonar Cut, with a sluice across a narrow neck of land between the river channels.

Looking round me, again, for I was approaching the mid-channel buoys, Essex bound, I chuckled, remembering a natty little dredger working in amongst a boatyard mooring trot while visiting Sandwich. "Just what's needed in our own moorings…" I'd said at the time to my mate. Sandwich had suffered much from siltation and died as a commercial port, except for pleasure craft. Crazy as it may seem, Sandwich was quite a busy port for the spritsail barge, some were even built here, *But turning one round now*…I thought, *might even be difficult*, while chuckling into the breeze.

I was clear now for some distance. No ship could cause me a hazard and there weren't any other yachts or powered craft to be seen either, so, yes, I was away, sailing down the River Stour again…

Suddenly remembering something funny, yet not really that funny, for Christobel got a bruised knee. On a later holiday based in that delightful coastal town of Deal in Kent, we had a jaunt out along the edges of the Ebbsfleet flatlands. The plan was to find the 'lost' port of Richborough. During the First World War, a huge munitions facility was built in Port Richborough, along with wharves and a roll on-roll off facility. The factory employed around nine hundred people, mainly women who were bussed in from all round the locality.

We'd parked up in the car park of a 'fast food outlet' to check on a route down to the water's edge. There was, but a gate was found to be locked! On the way back to the car, my good mate caught a foot in a tendril of brambles and took a 'flyer' landing badly and cutting her knee through her trousers. Ooops! Back at the car, we had a look. "Just a bit of a cut…" I said, gently, cleaning it with some antiseptic wipes.

The remains of the WW1 Port Richborough.

"I'm alright…but will need another pair of legs…" She'd changed out of a skirt earlier! A garage next door had a basic selection on offer.

After finding a different place to park, we 'fell' into a wildlife area which opened onto the river saltings. "Great," I said, "I can get along from here…" The mate declined to follow, being happy to wait.

I was soon traipsing round the rotting piles and concreted bases for heavy machinery. The remains of a jetty ran out obliquely to the current river edge, across the wide expanse of salt marsh. I was busy photographing when I saw the mate, leaning on a bit of the jetty. "I didn't want to miss out…" she said, "…my knee's alright…" That's my girl!

Troop and ammunition rains were rolled directly onto specially designed ships at the facility and offloaded over in Calais to be run towards the front lines. The first trains were loaded in February 1918, late in the conflict, but incredibly helpful in the efforts to bring it all to an end, surely. It was far ahead of its time and it wasn't until after the war that the system was used in the civil world. The machinery – span link – was unbolted and transferred to a new train ro-ro berth in Harwich harbour, where it remained in use until 1987. Its rusting structure can still be seen, unused, close by the Trinity House berth and buoy maintenance yard.

Port Richborough's ramp machinery at Harwich.

"Ah well," I said, "time to start thinking about heading home…" I had crossed the Ray Sands by that point and had the Essex Yacht Club's club ship on *Whimbrel's* nose. Tacking almost off the stern of the grey painted old minesweeper, I set a course for the tail of Canvey Island, the boat revelling in the course and breeze, virtually sailing herself.

The tide had turned but I had plenty of time. Time to look across the sparkling wavelets, far across the Thames highway, where the Yantlet ran falteringly in its 'death froes' out into the receding water's edge until it would dribble in a higgledy-piggledy fashion over the sands. Silted and essentially lost…

Coming in close to the saltings edge, I started the trusty diesel and tacked the boat into the wind. Letting sheets slack, I popped forward, ran the jib down, securing its head. Then I let the main rattle down too, throwing a few gaskets round it. *Fenders*...I thought, then said, with a more than a hint of self-admonishment, "Heck, nearly forgot those!"

As I pulled the mainsail cover on and began lacing it up, the kettle began to sing, so, being alone, I had to stop and 'drop' down into the cabin to shut the thing off! It hums and vibrates like the regenerative brakes of a modern train! It cannot be ignored. It drills through the senses!

Summing up mentally while sitting in the cockpit with my mug of tea...I felt exhilarated by the sail. It was grand, grand indeed. One thought lay unanswered though: would I one day sail to Sandwich? "I rather hope so," I said, laughing...

4
A Dabble Amongst the Western Isles

We were in the middle of breakfast one day, a few years ago now, my mate asked, "…any plans for your 60th?" Right out of the blue too. Of course, I hadn't a clue and shrugged. She looked quizzically at me and added, "You once mentioned a tall ship a while ago…" as if setting me up. I had indeed.

"I'll think about it, darling…" I murmured, looking at her, quickly casting such thoughts aside: 60 is a bit of a milestone and my mind was on a tide sail aboard *Whimbrel*.

The age of 60 may not be as big as it was a generation or two ago for, in the second decade of this millennium, one can expect to live a longer with a healthier active life, but, one can never be certain that a 'darkness' may not be so very far off…

Now, I must be honest, I'd always wanted to sail the Western Isles. This dates to my time as an engineer officer cadet serving aboard a Royal Fleet Auxiliary replenishment tanker posted to the Clyde areas to work with various submarines, training…the beauty of the probing lochs and craggy coastlines with their generally white sand beaches and deep green backdrops left a lasting imprint on my mind.

Time passed by and I received the perfunctory prod about whether I'd given any thought to my 'sixtieth' treat. I suppose, in a way, I had been doing so at the back of my mind: the thought about the Western Isles wish hadn't disappeared into the grey matter. I gave a perfunctory answer about still 'thinking' and…

But the penny had dropped. I knew, the where, I only needed, the how. Here, the wonders of technology that wasn't even a dream in my youth became my honed chisel as I pared my way down the layers of web grunge.

Outward-bound hiking, climbing and sailing between venue packages and copious numbers of trip yachts peeled off like shavings and I initially became disheartened: none of this was of interest. A couple of schooners and other luxuriant craft peeled away from the layers too. Then, I exhaled for before me was a picture that made the heart go bumpety bump. Before me was a strikingly pretty, yet unmistakably workmanlike gaff cutter, the *Eda Fransden*. "Nice…" I exclaimed, beaming already with excitement.

The *Eda Fransden* was built in Denmark in 1938 as a motorised fishing vessel with a small rig. During the 1980s she was acquired by a boat building family near Airor on the Knoydart peninsular, opposite Armdale on the Isle of Skye. The yard was in a cove a little to the south, at Doune Knoydart. Towards the end of her rebuild and remodelling from a motor-fishing vessel to passenger carrying gaff cutter, she was severely damaged in a fire. Amazingly, the craftsmen picked up their tools and restarted the job for the hull was so robust it was barely touched by the flames. The ship's owner at the time of my trip was a man with many sea miles under his belt.

The little ship measured 56 feet and 75 feet to end of her long bowsprit. Rigged as a gaff cutter, she came with a crew of three. She took eight passengers, in four small 2-berth cabins. Heaven!

"I've got it…" I bubbled to my mate over a cup of tea in the garden late in the autumn beforehand. I told her all about it.

Together we looked through the details. "Cabins look cosy," my mate said. Indeed, they did. In the eventuality, they were smaller and tighter than the internal plan seemed to indicate, but I'd already spotted that. I booked a cabin giving details about it being a '60th' treat. We had to answer loads of questions about whether or not we'd had any previous sailing experience. Lots of details about 'kit' and such issues. To make a package, we booked into a local hotel for a 'before and after' and two nights on Skye, Mull and a further two in Northumberland on the way home!

For a humble ditch-crawler, this was going to be a big departure from my norm, of my mate's too: we have an utterly deep-rooted love and affection for the little corner of England, bounded by the geographical limits of the Thames estuary between North Kent and Orford Ness mid-way up the Suffolk coast.

Time flew, our *Whimbrel* had been prepared ready for the season, her bottom anti-fouled and dry stores loaded ready. I was going to be 'unfaithful' for a while, I told her…the mate had a similar conversation on the last sail before heading north!

We arrived in Mallaig, the gateway to the Isles, west of Fort William, the day before staying at the lovely West Highland Hotel overlooking Rhum. Catching a glimpse of 'our' ship, I was, my wife said, "…like a little boy…" hopping up and down as 'Eda' floated serenely upon the harbour's translucent blue waters. I must have spent 15 minutes gazing upon her. Aboard, a member of the crew was busy doing some tidying – later I was to learn that the previous charter party had just cleared away…

The Eda Fransden serenely awaits in Malaig.

Now, anyone who has been to the West Coast of Scotland will know that the weather can be sublime, with soft breezes, and warm, like the gorgeous accent of the population. But, during the afternoon the wind 'piped up' with all the markings for a proper blow.

The early June weather had been diabolical across the whole of Britain and the tail end had yet to clear western Scotland. Ah, but it failed to dampen spirits!

Our boarding day, a Saturday, dawned wild and bleak. Looking to seawards from our hotel room, great baulks of water was crashing over a man-built rock edge bordering the seaward side of a carpark. White spume streaked inland!

After a hearty 'Scottish' breakfast, we went for a walk before organising ourselves. We joined a group of people all carrying various kit bags drifting along the marina pontoons walking towards our ship – our shipmates for the week, we deduced. It was still a grey afternoon, but I thought the wind had eased.

Once aboard, we were briefed and assigned cabins. Christobel looked at me as we stowed our bags, putting only our towels and flannel bags onto hooks on the bulkhead. The bags were left packed, to be used as our wardrobes. Hanging from clothing hooks were our lifejackets which we took up on deck, as instructed. Only a couple of people, I noticed, didn't know what to do with them and once we were all 'dressed' we were organised for departure. The skipper wanted to clear out, he explained, and motor to an anchorage in Loch Nevis where we would sit behind a protective headland for the night.

I must say, I was greatly impressed with the way the ship lifted and curtsied to the westerly rollers reaching across the Hebridean Sea. The anchorage was surrounded with a wild ruggedness, yet within its rocky bosom, we were cosseted like a babe within a womb.

Over a drink and meet chat, we all exchanged some biographical details. Our shipmates were a mix of people who had sailed on 'Eda' a few times, a couple who had never been afloat and us and alone, were boat owners. I could see that the crew were utterly sound. The ship's mate was a capable well-structured girl indeed. Amazonian, even, with an accent which spoke of the 'soft' home counties! Later, we found that she had attended a good private school in Kent, but sailing was her joy. While all of this was going on, the petite ship's cook continued with her work preparing our first dinner – delicious salmon cooked with wine, shallots and peppers, followed by blueberry cheesecake. The first of many exceptionally fine meals indeed…over fine food and wine, bonding was rapid.

Dinner over and the clearing up done and here I should add, we were all to take our turns with this during the week. Then, in what was clearly a well-honed system, the skipper briefed us on a flexible cruise with visits to sights of interest, 'bird' islands, breath-taking anchorages with due account of what the weather could be doing. However, a more settled spell was expected and our skipper was sure of a good week. First, the Treshnish Isles was planned and if there was a swell, he knew of a great a little anchorage, for our next night's ultimate destination.

The next day dawned grey with a westerly 5 to 6 with gusts. It ruffled the waters round our berth making our ship tug at her anchor. "Right," the skipper said, "…reef the mainsail." We were guided through it. The main was hoisted, three each to throat and peak. It was a big sail, so much easier on a spritsail barge from my own east coast of England! The jib was put in 'stoppers' ready for hoisting once an offing was gained. Helping to hoist the staysail, I remarked on sail names to my companion on the halyards: as a Bermudian sloop man, the foretriangle was either called a jib or foresail and, of course, there was the genoa which could be hoisted on the forestay instead…

Christobel looks aloft as we thrashed towards Ardnamurchan Point.

Once an offing was gained, the ready hoisted jib was set with a heave on a sheet. We were away, heaving the Scottish waters aside, sailing purposefully towards a distant Ardnamurchan Point, to leeward. At times, foaming water sluiced through the lee scupper. This was bloody grand stuff!

Turns at the wheel came and went as people desired. I was at the helm as we raced along past Rhum, Eigg and Muck. My trick lasted for a wonderful three hours, I was ecstatic with a perpetual grin… my good mate looked happy, nattering to a university lecturer from Sussex. A non-sailor, it turned out!

Rounding Ardnamurchan Point, we bore away to skirt down the outside of the Isle of Mull. The point seemed to bring a weather change for a once distant cloud line passed overhead and bathed our ship in sunshine. Then, the sea danced in varying hues of deep blues, reflecting the Atlantic sky. The rugged coast, a swathe of fantastic Scottish greens opened their glories. Gannets plunged for fish all round us. This was what I'd wanted.

The swell was too great to anchor among the Treshnish Isle,

so, we bore away for the island of Ulva, cocooned in the bosom of Mull. We worked in under sail, to an anchorage at Cragaig, I seem to remember. There was a big yacht flying the burgee of the Royal Northern and Clyde already sitting comfortably at anchor with its tender swinging astern. It looked a barren place, yet beautiful too in a rugged way.

We were soon ashore to look at the remnants of a once-thriving kelp milling industry. Kelp was once 'farmed' for it had the constituents for soap and fertiliser locked in. It was a prized commodity, especially during the Napoleonic wars and it was then that industries sprung up in many out of the way places. Back in 1845, 604 people resided on the island. Today, there are far fewer. A bothy stood close to the shore – these huts were available for hikers to use.

We wandered through the broken walls of a mill. Its old watercourse, still largely following mans directed route, chuckled through beds of flowering iris. We were staggered by the beauty of the place.

Ashore at an abandoned village on Ulva.

The ground was carpeted in swathes of scented bluebells, a good two months beyond those within the woodlands surrounding our Essex home. Profusions of sun-bright yellow iris straggled down to the tide lines amongst thick matted course grasses growing in the moistness. We saw wheatears mixed with oystercatchers and geese. A cuckoo called, then another, adding to the surreal feeling that surrounded us.

But a massive jaw jarring sight marred the natural environment, especially in any cove-like beach and that was plastic. It was spread thickly round the tide line and was scattered deep inland, windblown during high onshore gusts. "We should be ashamed…" I muttered as my mate too looked in horror. Fish boxes predominated with other fishing gear including coloured glass balls – southern European net floats we were told later.

Back aboard, the galley's earlier aromas had intensified as a slow-roasted leg of lamb appeared with Mediterranean vegetables. It was followed up by home-baked ginger shortbread with strawberries and cream…coffee and handmade truffles finished the meal.

It wasn't long before the first person slid away, tired and replete. It had been quite a day. My mate included. "I'm so tired…" she said smiling sleepily at me, "you have something first…" I went on deck with a glass of malt with a couple of our fellows and we nattered. It turned out that one had heard of me: he was an active fund-raiser for the Sea-Change Sailing Trust, as we were too!

The dawn caressed us with a barely perceptible westerly breeze. Bright and warm sunshine bathed the anchorage. It was beautiful. Breakfast over and washing up done – volunteers, one and all, by the week's end. The skipper called from the deck, "Right, we'll motor to the Treshnish Isles…then sail to Staffa…" We were all excited. Our first landing and a promise of puffins galore.

Puffins on Isle of Lunga waddled right up to us...

Off Lunga Island, where we were to anchor, puffins skimmed the sea's surface below the reflected sheer walls of rock that rose above. Above, a sea eagle soared majestically on the thermals, it was awesome and mesmerising. After a divine luncheon of mushroom risotto, the skipper relayed us ashore in Eda's rib, where we spread out following well-trodden pathways. Every now and then we stopped to admire clumps of pink thrift, primroses and bluebells clinging to any soil-filled cleft. Finally, we ascended to a grass carpeted cliff top.

This was puffin heaven. My mate sat back in a 'puffin trance' watching their landing antics – a totally ridiculous ungainly sight, something unappreciated from television views. They caused much mirth from our group. All about us a soft 'brrrrr-like' call emanated from the many burrows, seemingly shared with a race of rabbits with deep brown fur. If near a hole, puffins waited patiently for the trespasser to move before waddling indoors. Some just hopped over my mate's outstretched limbs. We were both elated.

The magnificent Fingles Cave on Staffa.

Our time quickly evaporated and below, as we returned to the beach, the harbour was filling with tourist boats! Anchor cleared away, we sailed serenely towards Staffa where Fingal's Cave would be our afternoon treat. The cave, formed from columns of volcanic basalt, has created an awe-inspiring natural and majestic cathedral. Two of our party sang a hymn, their voices grew in stature as nature's acoustics multiplied the sound. For me, it was strata formations of basalt rock with their acute and fantastic 'S' pathways, found closer to the landing point that gave me the greatest wow factor – something I remembered from a very distant geography lesson from a well-travelled schoolmaster!

From Staffa, in a steady breeze, we sailed for the southern tip of Mull. Bull Hole, under the little carrot-shaped island of Eilean nam Ban (Island of the women), where, it is said, Columba banished women here from Iona – what madness! We rounded under sail out of the Iona channel into a harbour of breath-taking scenic beauty. Watching the anchor fall to the bottom and hit the 'right' patch of sand clear of kelp was fascinating: in my own estuary waters visibility over two metres was rare. Soon, a party was preparing to go ashore onto the mainland of Mull.

My mate and I didn't go ashore, but for a while we sat, reading and talking over the day. The scenes witnessed, the sheer beauty of it all. Comparing, if one can, with the many east coast places we so love, each has its something – a something to be savoured. The whole day was a rolling conveyor; puffins; strange rocks; our ship rolling along through deep blue seas, lifting in genuflecting curtsies to the swell as she slipped gracefully along as if knowing where to go…

Returnees from ashore told of abandoned machinery and cottages. Later, I learnt that there was an abandoned mine ashore, its old, abandoned wharf still providing a landing place. Amazingly, it was from here that granite was mined for the building of Nelson's Column, Trafalgar Square. Pink granite was used to build the mighty Holborn Viaduct in London. Liverpool docks and various lighthouses of the 'Stevenson' design were built with the material too.

I later went ashore onto 'Eileen' with our skipper to catch the sunset over Iona. It had looked to be 'just one of those events in the event was a damp squib! After climbing a low hill covered in bracken to get the view, I was more struck by a verdant valley fit for grazing which lay within the island's hill fringed belly.

After another delicious meal, I savoured a wee dram on deck luxuriating in the evening's afterglow. Before sleep, I whispered to my dear mate, settling in her bunk above me, "I'm glad we did this dearest…" I wanted to climb up and join her – alas, space was tight!

What a week we were having: the settled spell continued. A glorious morning greeted us with the sun streaming down, evaporating the dew. Dally, we couldn't for we had to leave this idyllic spot. Assigned to assisting with hauling the anchor, I gazed into the water, glass clear and followed the cable to the bottom where it was lost amongst fronds of waving brown kelp, sailing in a tidal flow. Sail hoisted; the *Eda Fransden* frolicked in the conditions, surging in a slight swell. We were bound for Loch Sunart, on the underside of the Ardnamurchan peninsular, opposite Mull's north-eastern corner near Tobermory.

Along the way seals were profuse, popping up for air in the wake of our purposeful passage amongst these ancient isles. I went off with the skipper in the rib and we circled his lady. Wow, what a way to appreciate this voluptuous thing, a picture of pure poetry in sailing motion. Afterwards, a birding excursion was made skirting the shore of an aptly named island – the Dutchman's Cap. On Mull's mainland, sat an island castle, once the headquarters of an important clan, now empty other than history's echoes. Closing with a fishing boat, our ship's mate went away with £20, a bag of chocolate brownies and her scrumptious smile. She came back clutching dinner. Three huge crabs, two lobsters and her honour intact!

During the afternoon, with freed sheets and the staysail boomed out goose winging, we sailed along the top of Mull. We carried this into Loch Sunart where the high hills enveloped us, seemingly wrapping our ship within their fold, my mind crept into Stevenson's famous tale *Kidnapped* and of hiding from enemy clans of his saviour and British soldiers…

As we closed our night's anchorage inside the little island of Oronsay, the sail was gradually reduced. With a barely visible way ahead the skipper took us towards the shore, then, as if by some action of a magician's wand, the watery shaft known as Saileen Mor opened. The ship's mate was gazing intently into the depths. The bottom 'reared' up, alarmingly clear yet many metres below our keel. We swung and dropped our anchor close to one shore then a kedge was run onto the rocks astern, with a buoyed warp…

Ashore, at the headwaters, sat the remnants of a settlement with 'black' and 'white' cottages. With no sheep present, heather and bracken thrived and gullies were filled with spring green larch. My mate and I sat drinking in this anchorage, a place of great enchantment. By the end of our trip, it was the one that filled me with the most awe.

Sadly, our adventure was nearing its end, but in a morning full of glorious sunshine we motored in light winds until clear of Ardnamurchan Point, bound for the island of Canna. We hoisted that huge mainsail, then one sail after another, including the topsail.

Clearing the point, the skipper bore away and indicated for a relief. There seemed a dearth of volunteers, so I gladly took the helm for another long stint past Eigg, then Rhum with its tops shrouded in low cloud and towards distant Canna. On the way, the sea was peppered with great skuas. Dolphins were seen cavorting far away to one side of us, but they eschewed a visit.

Preparing light weather sails with the author feeding the jib out.

Passing Rhum, I asked the skipper a question about a strange building seen ashore – a building with what looked like columns. He dived below and came up with a book. "It's a family-run island…" he said, adding, "by the Bulloughs's." The building was a Doric columned mausoleum for deceased family members. The Island seemed severe on 'our' side. High cliffs with steep scree covered slopes and a green patchwork, except for a couple of low openings with no obvious harbour on this west facing shore.

As Canna's harbour opened, we tacked in, the skipper standing by one of our crew members for moral support: they hadn't wanted to do it! A few yachts were already at anchor and we rounded a little past a large yacht, with an equally large number of crew. Eda's rib was soon relaying us all ashore on the little adjacent island of Sanday which is connected to Canna by a causeway over tide washed rocks. We passed a deconsecrated church, St Edwards, under conversion to a study centre. It was an enjoyable walk, past a strung-out community.

In the 'town' itself one of two protestant churches was a visitor centre. We found a museum of island life in an old dairy which was fascinating to my mate as well as me. Ah, then we found the first café since departing Malaig. It was then run by an Englishman and a Slavic lady and the mix produced an enticing looking range of evening fare. Ah, but we were heading back for haggis and neaps! I awoke with a strange end of cruise feeling. It was our last full day. It struck me too that I was about to reach a personal milestone: It was the last day of my 50s too! But hey, a full-on life of sailing was still to be enjoyed.

Picturesque Canna Church almost melds into landscape.

Clearing Canna's wonderful little harbour, we set course for the Point of Sleat, the Isle of Skye's southern tip. We ran for hours. A huge pod of dolphins was sighted and chased to no avail. I was fascinated by Skye's Cullin Hills, '…arguably the finest range in Britain…', I was told. A few days later we were driving under the other side of them.

Sleat sat, seemingly, forever on our port bow imperceptibly getting slowly closer. As the afternoon drew on and the Point of Sleat fell astern, we lost our wind as the land shrouded us from the westerly that had wafted us along. At that timely point, the skipper fired up Eda's diesel and we motored towards Loch Nevis stowing and covering sails. It was a moment known well from our many cruises on *Whimbrel*: I looked at my mate. We both smiled, love emanating…

The *Eda Fransden* rounded to her anchorage and as her anchor splashed overboard for the last time, I gazed across the gorgeous blue water to a screen of white-painted houses peppering the shoreline beneath high wooded slopes of green in differing hues. I was mesmerised. So, this was Inverie, on the Knoydart peninsular, a community not connected by any road ashore: their local town was Malaig. We were all encouraged to go ashore. There are a few shops to wander round with one selling lovely local gifts. After a short walk, we fell into the remotest pub in Britain, for a celebratory drink.

I captured the 'Eda' under full sail.

The celebrations continued through dinner for my mate had secreted some bottles of 'bubbles' aboard earlier in the week, so I was toasted by our newfound shipmate friends and Eda's crew. It set us all up for a magnificent feast of French roast chicken followed by fruit crumble. Later, with the setting sun turning the harbour pink, I rounded off the last evening of my 59 years with malt or two!

Yes, it had been an exceptional experience greatly enjoyed. For my good mate, it was the puffins. For a little while we lay in our respective berths quietly comparing our love and affection for the low, yet oft pretty, silty estuary shores we knew so well with the dazzling brightness, sharp lines and clear seas of this glorious coast, vowing to come back…but before any further words were said, we were both overcome by sleep.

I awoke to being 60 years old. Above me, the sweet voice of my mate was softly singing, 'Happy birthday to you…' I was fed various small parcels and cards, from family too. Opening one, a shower of sparkles fell onto the cabin sole, some lodging in board cracks – sorry skipper! At breakfast, I wore a giant '60' badge and was congratulated.

We motored in an oily calm, cutting wooded reflections from the high hills as we crossed to Mallaig. Once moored, a fine birthday cake appeared and as I made the first cut, all and sundry began singing the traditional song. It was brilliant.

Knoydart Harbour in a reflective mood...

I felt proud of our crew: courteous, caring and fun throughout. I thanked them all for their week of friendship.

So, our wonderful dalliance amongst the Western Isles, ended.

Notes: Yarn was first told in a much-reduced version published in Yachting Monthly, December 2016, An East Coast sailor discovers Scotland's Western Isles.

Yes, we went back for more the following year to celebrate my sister's coming of age too!

5
Waiting for the Tide...

It was during a summer cruise and we were in the northern area of the Thames Estuary when 'waiting for the tide' took on a whole new meaning for *Whimbrel*'s crew. Something we have remembered with a mixture of hilarity and seriousness.

Parts of this tale appeared in Yachting Monthly, July 2015, in a very much reduced manner as 'Mortified off Mistley' and I feel the whole story should be told for as my mother candidly said to me once, "You always tell the truth..." Right!

We were anchored deep up Landermere Creek amongst the salt-washed saltings, close enough to savour the heady saline scents. It was a favoured spot, 'far from the madding crowd' with rarely another boat in that leg of the creek to make the anchorage seem crowded.

On the tide, local boats come and go from Landermere Quay and during the afternoon we'd enjoyed seeing the converted lifeboat *Stenoa* return to her moorings just below the old quay. The little ship is a glorious sight under sail and we had been well rewarded in our position. During the afternoon, I had been for a 'spin' in the tender, sailing round the underside of Skipper's Island, nosing amongst the salting edges, investigating old docks.

Over afternoon tea we discussed the next few days. The mate had said to me that our provisions needed to be topped up and Manningtree is an easy place to do this, providing you are of a moderate draft. The Stour was agreed. We'd four or five days left to potter before heading down to the River Blackwater area, so a night either side of 'Manningtree' somewhere within the border river between Essex and Suffolk was our plan, leaving a stop-over at Harwich's useful Halfpenny Pier as a jumping-off point. The town always delights.

The following morning dawned fine with a purposeful south-westerly, filling me with unabated joy. The settled spell of weather that had persisted for some time was continuing unabated. So, as planned, a 'run' up the delightful River Stour was our day's plan.

The day's journey would only be to Wrabness, for from a mooring under the delightful sandstone strata cliff we relish the challenge of sailing on the early flood up the twisting headwaters of the river past Mistley Quays into Manningtree. We normally fetched up on one of the Stour Sailing Club's visitor buoys, off their hard, giving easy access. Ashore, a varied mix of stores abound, as well as several enticing café's and, of course, a fine public house serving good grub overlooking the moorings.

Following me into the cockpit, the mate said, 'Normal procedure?' I nodded, adding a couple of comments.

The anchor cable was shortened and cleared away. With sails ready for hoisting, the anchor was broken out and hauled in. The jib was hoisted and we were away. While the mate crept round the closest point into the run of the creek with several moorings within, I sluiced the chain and let it below. Clearing the moorings, the mate shot the boat into the wind as I hauled the main aloft. Regaining her course, we were under sail properly and forging over the still ebbing tide.

In Hamford Water, I could see a boat not lying to her anchor as she should. "Aground…" I said pointing. The mate looked at me: the bottom in this upper section of Hamford Water has become rippled with underwater hummocks waiting to trap the unwary. The shallows ran towards the entrance to Kirby Creek. As if to drive home the matter, we kissed a mud hump and slowed. The boat's momentum carried her through under the press of the kindly south-westerly.

Away along the broken edge of Garnhams Island, waders were skittering along the uncovered mud below the breeze ruffled salting banks. Here and there a view into the mid-lands of the island was glimpsed. Once used for sheep grazing, it has long been flooded and was used by Arthur Ransome in his Secret Water (a book based upon the Backwaters) and was the last part to be explored by the Swallows and Amazons group of children before the 'mother ship' returned to collect them all.

It was an easy sail to Harwich harbour then a beat, with the flood, in long and shorts up to the Wrabness moorings. "Take your pick…" a friendly yachtsman called as I was about to ask. We did.

It was a delightful sail upriver, surprisingly further than many sailors think, about five sea miles, to what I call this 'halfway' point, but was somewhat greater what with the tacks. We love this stretch of water, but it's not a place to stay during a strong easterly or westerly. The sister counties of Essex and Suffolk are grand vistas to gaze upon, with the Royal Hospital School above Holbrook Bay as a particular spectacle.

The next day dawned with a steady, but light, north-westerly which later became an easterly sea breeze! "Breakfast...then off," I said, returning below after finishing my post ablutions cuppa.

Leaving, under sail, we chatted about this and that. Of old disused wharf stumps and the bottoms of a disintegrated old spritsail barge. The mate asked about the rusted remains on Wrabness Beach. Her colours mimic those of the cliffs above her, but, sadly, I had to admit to knowing nothing about her other than that she was clearly not an old iron-pot sprittie.

Early on the tide sailing past Mistley with Swan Bank beyond.

The north-westerly was kindly direction, we had to tack, yes, but the last leg had the wind on our beam. Going down past Mistley's quays, we lost the wind while tacking close into 'Swan' Bank – a delightful spot covered with roosting swans as soon as the tide dropped sufficiently. During neaps, it is only partially covered. It was something to be avoided!

"Okay, start the engine," I said, adding, "the next leg is into the wind…I'll stow sails." The engine was engaged. Leaving the mate to it, I stowed our sails and we pottered up to the Stour Sailing Club's visitor moorings. After a quick tidy, the tender was pulled alongside.

Alighting from our tender, the mate said, "Stores, then lunch." It was a decision! We ambled through the town, a place oft visited, shopped, collecting more than was listed and headed back to the waterfront where we knew a light baguette lunch could be enjoyed. I had a glass of beer. Dizzy Blonde it was called – very tasty indeed! (Here lies a tale: some years earlier I had come in here with a friend. We'd had a glass of the same beer and in the evening later that day, I said to my mate, tongue in cheek, "I had a dizzy blonde today…there was a long silence." Then the penny dropped, with much hilarity!)

Returning aboard, the boat had swung to a steady easterly. I grinned at my mate and said, "We'll look at Wrabness, or those shallows off Stutton Ness," thinking of our comfort. With sails set, the mate sailed us off, following the general run of the buoyed channel. On a leg towards Mistley, for some unknown reason, I took the helm. The mate kept saying, "You can sail her higher than me…"

Ignoring the perfect line being taken, I hardened up without proper due attention…Big mistake: as the centre plate cut through mud, I leapt to the plate winch and wound a couple of turns. Okay. Then a scrunching shingly sound erupted. We stopped with a jerk! Why I hadn't put the helm over, I will never know. Complacency? I immediately saw that we were sitting by Swan Bank, on the wrong side of a steep shingle mound bordering the deep-water channel.

"Bugger," I said, starting the engine and attempting to turn the boat away from the western tail of Swan Bank. The boat moved, stopped, moved again before stopping. I went forward leaving my mate to thrust ahead, we bumped further around before stopping again. I dumped the sails.

"I'm going overboard," I called, stripping off my life jacket for it would have erupted into life. By getting my back under the curve of *Whimbrel's* stem, the boat shifted round a little further, but it was no good: the tide was visibly dropping away from a bank now showing itself in all its glory. Swans paddled close by, looking on inquisitively. "Shut engine down…" I called, adding, "come over and give me a hand."

In the shallows, we heaved the bow round, but the stern was fast…ashore a lady was shouting at us. I waved and took no notice. The water was just over our knees by then. It was all up!

I cursed the predicament I'd got us into. I looked at my mate and said, "Sorry…" She smiled. After getting back aboard using the transom ladder, she let the anchor go with a load of cable. The anchor was laid out later towards the receding line of the tide, away from the darned bank.

"Chuck me the broom…I'll make myself useful…"

"Did you see that person calling out?" the mate asked, handing me the broom. I hadn't and not thinking about her any further, I brushed off the boat's bottom as one side came up as she settled over towards the bank. As I moved round the stem and did what I could reach, I had a sense of being watched…

I looked with horror when rounding the bow for I found myself looking into the faces of several black visor helmeted Royal National Lifeboat Institute personnel…and the Harwich Inshore Lifeboat…

Walking towards the closest, I said, cheerily, "Hi, is there something I can do for you…?" I then became aware of the persistent whirring of an emergency siren ashore. A coastguard Land Rover was seen screeching to a halt over on the quay. Ashore a small crowd had gathered and the cameras were busily clicking.

The lifeboat crew wanted to attempt to pull the boat off. I told them quite bluntly that they were to do no such thing. We were listed over and fast. I said, "You'll pull the deck out of her…"

"She'll move," one said. So, I reiterated my no you will not, saying we'll float on the next tide!

I was a chastened skipper that afternoon and during the evening after managing to cook a decent meal: we'd plenty of fresh food. Plates? No! I used our big pasta bowls which just held to the table mats without sliding.

The morning's tide was about the same level as the one we grounded on. I was a little concerned and silently prayed it would make as predicted. During the afternoon I'd called the coastguard to advise of our position (which they already knew about) and said we would call when clear. It was to fulfil a request left with us by the departing lifeboat crew.

It was a bit of a torrid sleep we gained upon the berths and I was glad when I heard the first of the tide's slaps under the 'flat' bottom. The tide had arrived. We got up and had a coffee. Outside, it looked glorious. There was a bit of a moon and stars could be seen in a profusion away from it. The shoreside lights lit the way we would need to go – but first, we needed to float.

Eventually, I went into the cockpit and looked at the level on the rudder. Daft: the boat hadn't even begun to pick up.

I heard my mate asking, "Another coffee?" It helps time run on…

The boat shivered and lifted. We were upright again. I looked over the transom and saw the level was creeping over the forward running curve of the blade. I looked at the time. Just under an hour to high water…"I think we'll be alright," I said softly to my mate who was sitting on top of the centre plate case, adding, "I'll go forward and pull on the cable." There would be slack from picking up. I took it in and went back aft.

A stirring was felt. "She's moving," the mate said, full of unbounded optimism. I felt it too.

Going forward the cable had slackened. I took the strain, the boat moved. Looking aft, I said, "Start the engine…gently ahead…" I took in the chain with a feeling of pure joy with more than a tinge of excitement. The anchor came up and I housed it. I ran the cable below and went aft. The mate was steering towards deeper water and we 'hit' the channel near an old disused wharf at the Manningtree end of Mistley's quays.

Taking the helm, I steered carefully down the run of the quays, then away down the line of red and green blinking navigation buoys – our passage to freedom.

"We'll creep into the anchorage off Stutton Ness," I said, giving my dear mate's arm a squeeze. There wasn't a breath of air. The previous evening's sea breeze had evaporated during our waiting hours. It was essentially idyllic, sort of romantic, gliding downstream over the last of the flood.

I could see the beacon to the south of Stutton Ness, but there was a bright steady light to its north. What? Closing where we soon needed to turn in towards the Ness's shore, I spotted the 'what' a Thames barge was in the anchorage, resting gently, silhouetted in the moonlight, its crew oblivious to the clinker hulled yacht creeping in.

It was with great relief that the anchor splashed overboard. The chain was paid out, snubbed and more let go. We were safely at anchor, swinging to the ebbing tide.

As I set the anchor ball and the lit riding light, the mate, with a voice full of love and caring, called, "flavoured coffee, come on…"

Sipping and looking at her, I could see the relief that I was feeling too. "Yes," I said gently, adding, as my eyebrows raised a little, "what an eventful day on the Stour we've had…"

My mate looked at me, the look said it all!

What the log said: After the earlier events etc. "Terrible Tuesday…That night, at 0254, we swung to our anchor, motored down to Stutton Ness, re-anchored and slept!"

6
A Siblings' Sailing Romp

In the same year that I was diagnosed with prostate cancer, the eldest of my two brothers, Graham, had a long arranged and well-planned visit back 'home' from Newfoundland, Canada.

It was at least six months beforehand that he called to say he'd be over during the year. "It'll be in late August…" he said, laughing, with clearly a note of something not yet told. Then, about the timing, he explained, "I looked at the tide tables for Southend…for sailing see…" Another laugh, before adding, "Then I booked my flights…"

"Ah, right…" I said, "I'll make sure we're home!" chuckling, but thinking, once a sailor, always a sailor, in body, mind and soul!

Meanwhile, following the last of a series of appointments for my prostate cancer, we had the uninterrupted remainder of that year's summer sailing on our own.

So, much closer to the time, because our sister, Theresa, hadn't been able to have 'her' week sailing aboard *Whimbrel*, I asked if she'd like to come along. She jumped at the chance the moment I mentioned it. Getting a word in edgeways, I added, "It'll be a five-day heist round the Thames Estuary…come the day before." And so, it was all arranged.

On the day that our elder brother was due to arrive for his stay, Theresa drove up from her home a little earlier, in time to help store ship. A selection of ales from a fine Wiltshire brewery arrived too, I was glad to see!

The call came through and our brother was duly picked up from the train station. After some tea, he was whisked off by Theresa to get some essential stores, they said. I never got to the bottom of what happened: she 'allowed' him to overindulge the collection of bottles gathering in their trolley with enough beer to sink the Titanic! Laughing about it a year later, I was told, 'He kept adding bottles…' Siblings, eh! After it was stowed aboard, the following day, it lasted into the early weeks of the next season. Cheers dear brother!

Essential stores come aboard!

We had a typical 'family' evening with the usual chaffing soon flowing. A pair of roasted chickens provided a feast in which our boy joined his aunt and uncle in all but demolishing. It must be said, as we toasted the cruise, we all wished the youngest of our siblings could have been along for the trip too. Next time, perhaps.

The next morning, I was making noises early to stir the crew into a semblance of order. Theresa's car was used to transport us to the creek. After preparing and leaving the dinghy on the club's slip, we all headed for *Whimbrel* to get the final stores aboard. Both headsails were fetched out and the genoa was rigged for use, whilst the jib was neatly stowed along the port guard rail. Graham was tasked with fetching the dinghy – his first foray afloat for two years! On his return, the mainsail was ready for hoisting too.

Over a coffee, it was time for a briefing, rather than the plan sketched out the previous evening…I had ready prepared our passage plan a couple of days earlier after checking the expected five-day weather picture. That done, I said, "Right…we'll slip out and hoist sail as we go…" We had a mere few minutes to wait before the boat lifted.

One of the things I warned my siblings about was the fact that my medication often made me tired during the afternoon. So, after a very uneventful passage round the Maplins, down the Swin to the Swin/Wallet Spitway, where the only excitement was Graham washing up our lunch things and passing the spritsail barge *Cambria*, we scurried into the Colne. The day had started a little overcast with a decent breeze, but the sun came out and we enjoyed excellent conditions for a coastal sail. Coming off the wind, *Whimbrel* enjoyed the full power of that breeze going up the Colne. Clearing Mersea Stone, we all looked towards two sailing barges with their cocky sprits and lofty topmasts piecing the sky. 'Which ones?' I was asked.

"The *Thistle* and *Kitty*..." I said, laughing for I knew they wanted to catch me out. We'd had a discussion over our sighting of *Cambria* earlier! I was right!

"How do you know?" Graham asked.

"Just does..." Theresa quipped.

"Well, it's easy really..." I said, "look at them..." pausing while they looked. "One is painted green also has a star in her topsail..." We couldn't see the latter, but it's on her bob too.

"I remember Kitty," Theresa said chuckling.

"So," I said, "the other has a high peaked bow and a wheelhouse." Pointing at her, "and she doesn't have a mulie mizzen, look closely..." She often looks odd, so rigged, for she is a relatively large barge, with a bow sprit too. (A mulie mizzen is a gaff and boom rigged sail, rather than the traditional sprit and boom for a Thames barge's aft sail)

Sailing into Pyefleet at end of the first day…

We were entering Pyefleet Creek by then. It was at that point I went forward and ranged some metreage of anchor chain on the foredeck. The anchor was unlashed ready to drop, after we'd rounded up. Back aft once again, I briefed my crew about rounding up on my mark and for the sails to be lowered. As I finished speaking, the wind puffed and veered. "Creek bend…" I said, chuckling. It happened again after a short return to where it should have been – right on our beam. As we heeled even further, from forward, the unmistakable noise of fast 'running' chain reached my ears…

I shot bow-wards, arresting the run with a foot and grabbed the cable. "Luff up," I called loudly for we were sailing too fast to haul in. As the boat slowed, I hauled the chain in quickly, hand over hand, feeling rather chaste. "Okay," I called aft, grinning. Amazingly, there wasn't a mark on the deck or, more to my delight, on the varnished rubbing band. The chain had literally flown!

I stayed forward. Reaching a 'happy place' I signalled to come up into the wind. The anchor was let go, cable paid out, snubbed and let go more, by which time the jib was down and main was following. "Four times the depth," I said, going aft, smiling as I saw the entry being made by my sister into the log.

Settling over tea, I said, I was tired. "Yes," the two chimed in unison. "No damage," my sister added, "is the main thing…" We all laughed. The worst hadn't happened…anchor catching the bottom and bringing boat up hard!

My sister, bless her, had come prepared for the evening's meal. Three superb pieces of rib-eye steak with a potato and broad bean salad. Simple. It was washed down with a glass or two of red. Christobel had sent us off with three home-produced sticky toffee puddings – these were enjoyed with clotted cream. By then, the evening had drawn in. It was sublime with an oil lamp illuminating the cockpit as we sat nattering.

Next morning, we awoke to a westerly. I beamed at the crew. We all knew we were in for a grand day of sailing. Soon after nine, sail was set and we were away, running out of Pyefleet. The first of the ebb was caught going down the Colne. "We'll cross the bar under the point," I said, reminding all of the passage plan discussed over breakfast. The helm nodded, before reaching over and tweaking the satnav. "Just beyond No. 1," I said, grinning at my sister, adding, "you've done it a few times…" She looked at me with a knowing smile, for she too was probably remembering conversations with another crew of ours.

It was a grey morning and our oilies were in use to keep out a bit of a chill. With a brightness beyond the Naze, we passed the striking spritsail barge *Melissa* with her rust-red hull and black rails.

By two we were rattling into Harwich with shafts of sunshine flecking the harbour wash waves. Soon we were up to the hills, which always remind me of the lithe curves of fine sculptured women, bordering the River Orwell on both sides below Levington. Then, rounding Collimer Point, with Pin Mill hard on the port bow, the sun was serenading our arrival in full force. Both of my crew were entranced. Graham hadn't been to this little port for some years, Theresa, well, she could tick off on her fingers the times she'd visited, much to her eldest brother's disgust!

Our Pin Mill tea!

While the two crew took it in turns to potter off in the dinghy, I took the opportunity for a little snooze. Upon waking, tea had been cleared and my crew were thinking about their meal ashore. "A beer?" Graham said coyly as he licked his lips as if in appreciation of a sip!

"You lot get it organised," I said, cheerily, refreshed from my sleep, adding, "I'll check the weather for tomorrow…" Wow. It had changed somewhat in a short space of time. "Look," I said, with a touch of earnestness, "I think we ought to make a whole day passage to the East Swale tomorrow…" I showed the crew the forecast for the following night. "Come from nowhere…" I muttered, "…not looking brilliant for late summer!"

"Hmmm…" Was my sister's reaction, a qualified skipper, followed by, "Yes!"

So, leaving them, I sat and prepared a passage plan for the East Swale. The Colne or Blackwater were alternatives. The wind, a north-westerly, would be favourable. Our departure was going to be at four in the morning, in darkness.

"We'll have an hour and half of ebb…" I said, "…get clear of the harbour…"

So, we were soon setting off for the hard. The Butt and Oyster was our target for some supper. The tide was rising so Graham was detailed off as 'dinghy boy' meaning it was his job to pop down every now and then to fetch her up a bit!

The pub was a little quiet for the time of year I thought, but its atmosphere was to par. We sat at a table with a view over the hard. The hard has changed a bit over the last few seasons. A fresh shingle layer has been laid and a couple of old barge hulks were re-floated and moved downriver to join a collection of other vessels under the trees to act as a 'bind' point for a protective fringe of saltings to develop for the hills have been 'sliding into the sea' along that section for some time.

The alarm shrieked a little before four. Mutterings came from the adjacent berth as I swung my legs out from my bunk on the port side of the fore cabin and shrugged into my shorts. I grabbed my oily bottoms from the hook behind the loo door and went through to the main cabin to put the kettle on, rousing the other semi-alert befuddled crew. Sliding the washboards out, I went into the cockpit and felt the late summer early morning chill bite. It was dark, very dark, with just the odd shore lights, apart from flashes from buoys upon the river, gleaming onto yacht hulls intermittently.

The dinghy had been prepared, with mast lashed in its stowed position, upon our return from ashore. We'd had a quick coffee and nothing more before sleep, in anticipation of a long day. "Make the drinks," I called below, "while I free things up round the boat." I released the halyards, removed most of the sail lashings and dropped off the mooring, leaving our line ready to slip. I prepared the jib rather than genoa in line with expected conditions.

Two sleepy-looking heads met me on my return. The kettle had just boiled. The tea was in the pot. "Quiet…" a voice from below broke the silence. I nodded, but no one saw.

"We'll have to use power to get away," I said. "We'll set the main though." As we drank the scalding tea, we discussed issues. "Breakfast," I said, "needs to be had before any wind comes."

"I'll do it outside Harwich…" Theresa offered; in a kind of

maternal-sisterly fashion, she had adopted for my brother and me.

We cleared the moorings and gave ourselves manoeuvring room. In the cockpit's port corner, the satnav map glowed brightly, too brightly, for it interfered with my eyes, so I fumbled in the darkness with the 'off' button and reduced its intensity. "That's better…" I heard from behind an ear.

"More tea anyone," I chirped, knowing the answer, so added, "I'll make it…"

We were soon rounding Collimer Point and the reflected light from Felixstowe's Trinity Port, where huge container ships came and went in a continuous seamless stream, lit the dawn prematurely. Further east though, the real dawn was creeping inexorably across the night sky, beating it back in a slow waltz.

By the time Harwich Harbour was reached we were into a dawn sky. It wasn't until clear of the harbour's eastern land edge at Languard Point that we experienced its full grandeur. Off the boom end, an orange glow was eating upwards into a clear sky. The sky had signs of being a very blue one indeed with not a cloud to be seen, yet a haziness hung on the horizon. Changes and some cloud later, I thought. More wind too.

Sunrise came as we reached across Pennyhole Bay.

"Cor, that's good…" my brother and I chorused together as bacon rolls were handed out from below, followed by sauce containers. We all munched with contentment as the boat virtually looked after herself, on a reach towards the Naze.

We passed the Naze around two hours after our departure. The tide was then helping us along, but would, at some point be against us. The boat was revelling in the conditions, as were the crew. I looked out at them from the galley whist clearing the breakfast debris. It would be the last clear up until much later!

It wasn't long before cloud was beginning to build round the horizon's edges as the darkened sky of the early hours became the morning proper. I listened to the forecast on the VHF radio, saying to my crew, "We'll need to reef at some point." We discussed this and decided not to reduce sail while going along so nicely. The land was getting further away as we made a course directly for the Wallet Spitway and after clearing 'Frinton' we were more 'at sea' and closing the giant wind turbine farm on the Gunfleet Sands. Strangely, those turbines gave a sense of security, however falsely!

"Right," I said, "I'll put the first reef in…" It was all done at the mast. At the appointed moment, the designated crew eased the mainsail until it was no longer filled. I topped the boom up and hauled in the outer reefing line and then pulled the sail's luff down, attaching the foot eye to its hook. Releasing the boom downhaul, I swigged the hoist tight and tensioned the luff again. Lastly, dropping off the topping lift and tweaking the kicker – all done. Looking aft, I saw the mainsheet was being pulled in.

Back aft again, I looked aloft at the sail's set, before turning to my siblings, saying, "That's better," and grinning, for my stress had gone. The boat felt it too and no speed had been lost either.

We settled again with the wind turbines close away to our port side. A boat, we'd picked up earlier far off, was closing rapidly on a reciprocal course. "We have right of way…" Theresa said to Graham who was at the helm. I smiled, without turning, leaving them to it. I was watching clouds of sparkling sun-drenched droplets falling like twinkling stars from the spray being thrown up by the bow. It was a pretty sight, everchanging! The boat's clinker hull was scrunching though the now short waves and the cabin 'pinged' resonantly to my watchful ears in the cockpit.

By the time we were closing the Wallet Spitway, I was helming. Theresa had gone below, for what, I wasn't sure. Graham was looking below, amused by something, so I bent forward and saw she was trying to close a locker door. I knew what had happened for it occurs frequently! If something goes between door and locker, the door clicks open when the boat hits a sea! She was trying to shovel my 'boxers' back into their cupboard. Seeing a bigger sea coming, I called out, "Leave it, watch out…"

As I concentrated on a series of seas, building up as we neared the shallows of the Spitway, I lost sight of what was happening below. There was a silence. Too much of a silence. "Graham," I said, "go and look…"

"Hit her head…" I heard drifting up from the cabin.

"Is she alright?"

There was a 'deafening' silence.

After a mere moment, I called urgently, "What's happened," adding, "do we need to change course?" thinking of running up to

Brightlingsea for medical assistance, or whatever…

Graham reappeared. "She's bleeding," he said, "hit her head… she's sort of grinning though…"

"Here, take over, keep her as she is."

Below, Theresa had a wadge of tissue in her hand and was holding it to the back of her head. Gingerly parting her hair, I looked closely. "Scuffed…" I said, grinning, a bit of blood though, "but how do you feel, dizzy, sick…" She looked at me painfully, trying to explain but finished with a smile.

"I'm alright," she said as if to reassure me.

"Okay, I don't think we need to change course…I'll mop your hair and you can sit in a downside corner where we can see you…"

"Outside," she said bravely, and then made her way back to the cockpit.

The steep sea had quietened, so I put right the problem's cause, ensuring the locker outer door was properly closed. Back on deck, I saw my sister's complexion had lost its 'weather beaten look' and was an insipid paleness. I'm sure she was more hurt than was ever likely to let on, but we could watch her easily from her safe corner.

Romping across the estuary…

I regained the helm too, as we sped towards the Wallet Spitway buoy, its clanging clearly telling of its presence. The tide was sluicing past it, running in a westerly direction across the sands with some two hours of flood remaining.

We held a course, after clearing the Swin Spitway buoy, almost on a par with the Wallet one, 'eating up' the Swin, rapidly, with that tide still with us. Overhead, sunshine beamed down from a largely clear sky. The clouds were still holding back on the horizon's fringes. As the boat danced to the Swin's waves, I was momentarily entranced by colours capering in unison on the varnished main hatch. I couldn't dwell on this for looking at where we were, I knew a tack would be needed to clear the foot of the Barrow Sand, so making a snap decision, I said, "We'll cut through the Barrow," adding, "there is a gap here now…used it before…" I explained further.

The foot of the Barrow Sands had split and become a 'lump' of sand where the mate and I have often seen seals basking, during the short period the sands were visible at the bottom of the ebb. So, from near the East Maplin buoy area, we sailed serenely through, with Theresa watching the GPS map and Graham the depth. Within a trifle, we were into the deeper water edging the Barrow Deep – free to romp southward.

It was Graham's trick at the helm by then and we had an amazing sail, a roaring broad reach across the estuary. It took around an hour, by which time our 'injured' crew was looking much better with full colour back in her cheeks. As time went on, in the fashion of 'well set' siblings, much chaffing soon started to ebb and flow. With some mirth the cabin side edge, down below, was even inspected for damage!

As the Red Sands World War Two Maunsell Forts approached, our sister said, "I'll make some tea…" and before either of us could object, she was below filling the kettle. Soon, slabs of fruit cake were passed out, followed by three steaming mugs. Munching and sipping, we sailed on. The boat had been going at nigh on maximum speed for hours. What a difference it made in eating up all those sea miles. By noon, the old forts were passed by and I had my mind fixed on the Middle Sand and then the Columbine Spit.

With a second mug of tea inside her, Theresa 'insisted' on having her stint on the helm and Graham, as always, very reluctantly relaxed his hold on the tiller, joint holding it for a few moments. Sis was back in charge!

Reaching well to the west of the Columbine Spit buoy, we hardened up. The tide was by then running out and had been for an hour or so before. Some tacks were made and we weathered the Pollard Spit. I looked at the time, then at my two crew. It had been a long day. 'Okay, I'll stow the jib…we'll motor-sail this last bit.'

Two hours later sis was back 'in charge…'

Quite a thrust was needed to 'break free' of the outer fast running body of water. Once past Shell Ness and the old white painted Coast Guard cottages, the water's surface was merely ruffled and we cantered along over the ebb. Down past the Sand End buoy marking the hard edge of the Horse Sand, seals in large numbers were being seen. I pointed out the rotting hulk of the spritsail barge *New World* in its muddy grave over on the Harty shore, briefly explaining its function as a submarine boom winching base during World War Two.

Before we passed Faversham Spit, I stowed the mainsail and

set a mooring line and the boathook ready, forward. We were soon moored to a friend's buoy, with 'permanent' permission to use, if empty of his own boat, upstream of the Harty Ferry hard along the mainland shore. The chap's main mooring was located inside Oare Creek.

While I was tidying round the decks, tea was made. No sooner than it had been consumed, a sailing pal ranged alongside in his dinghy. I wasn't the best of hosts: I was SO TIRED! My crew made most of the running. Moments after the chap departed, I was 'sent to my bunk' and told to rest.

I was woken, sometime later to the sounds of mirth and laughter, and 'you didn't…'

Rubbing my eyes, I realised I was still wearing my peaked sailing hat. As I swung my legs off the bunk there was more laughter. Going through, I was 'shocked' to be shown a picture of me asleep, blissfully unaware of what my siblings were up to. It went viral on our family messenger page. Ha-ha! They had at least done all the washing up…

From our cockpit, in a semblance of late afternoon summer sunshine, we were entertained by a friend's sea scout group sailing into the anchorage. Orders floated across the water as the boats shed sail, heading towards the hard where some people were clearly awaiting their arrival for trailers were being trundled down to the water's edge.

While I was preparing our supper, surreptitiously I wrote a 'post-it' note. I stuck it to the varnished cabin side where Theresa earlier 'bonked' her head. It said, "Damaged by Theresa, dated August."

"What…" my sister said later, screwing up her face and gently feeling the back of her head. It caused much mirth amongst the three of us, as we toasted our passage! It has continued to do so…

For supper, I cooked up pasta with a puttenesca sauce, served with salad. It was a good nutritious meal, much enjoyed by all.

The next morning, we all awoke after a very deep sleep indeed. A casual breakfast was enjoyed before slipping our mooring and we sailed west, making long and short tacks along the mid-body of The Swale. The reef from the previous day was kept in the mainsail to ease sailing. Above, scattered puffy clouds skittered across the blue sky giving intermittent sunshine. It had been a wise move to 'come all the way' the previous day, we all thought.

The spritsail barge *Greta* had motored past us down near Elmley Ferry and we met her again, preparing to make a U-turn in the waterway, below Ridham Docks. She had a large party aboard, sightseeing and bird watching probably.

"Better call Kingsferry Bridge," I said, adding we're 20 minutes away now. Theresa made the call. Amazingly, the bridge opened as we came up towards it and we sailed through with our engine running on tick-over.

The birdlife which always builds up during the summer was quite stupendous. It was a delight to see avocet clustered on edges. Oystercatchers squabbled on the saltings seemingly in open battle with their fellows. Shelduck and grebes were seen and the sounds of curlews added to calls floating in the air.

Clearing Long Point, the jib was stowed and we sailed down wind into Queenborough Harbour, where the previously fluky wind was a steadier north-westerly. Fluky airs are 'normal' under the back of Rushendon Hill. I called up the harbour office. "Normal side," the voice crackled back, "any one you like…" Theresa was dispatched forward to be ready to hook the buoy line. Closing with it, Graham inadvertently began the dropping mains'l too early. "Oi," I called loudly, as he rapidly hauled it sufficiently up again. Then, without any further hitch, we sailed onto the buoy, and it was deftly hooked by the crew.

"Well done…" I said, chuckling.

"Now for some tea…" I heard, whilst coiling the halyards off at the mast.

My crew picking up a mooring buoy under sail.

It wasn't long before the harbour boat ranged alongside with one of the usual friendly faces grinning across at us. Having paid the dues, well, I think my sister did, we booked a 'going ashore' time.

Over a beer, we chatted about the ease and comfort of the day's sailing, even though conditions dictated the keeping of the reefed mainsail. The Swale is like that. Unless a howling easterly, or westerly, the main body running east/west can be sailed in comfort in a bit of a blow. The north/south bends too if you're intent on enjoying sailing, as we were. There was none of the short nastiness and sometimes heavy water of the day before.

A couple of jars were enjoyed in Admiral's Arm before dinner with champagne at the Queen Phillipa. Theresa and I had a small issue with an overcooked dish, but it didn't spoil the event. Some years earlier, the 'Phillipa' a down at heel 'music pub' was known as the place to go if wanting a 'spliff' or more, until it was shut down! It is now a bijou mini-hotel with bistro type dining.

In the morning, we were away by seven, sailing off the buoy, under full main and the Genoa. We ran out with our bacon sizzling under the grill. It was a simple sail, across Thames, but the forecast spoke of more wind. It wasn't until we were beyond Southend Pier and into the Ray channel that it arrived, almost too much for the sail we had set. But what fun the crew had!

Coming across the Thames though, the sight that had my sister and I in stitches for quite some time was of our brother, literally scrubbing the cooker top with a wire wool cleaner and polishing it. He did a grand job, as the ship's mate later testified!

Near Southend Pier we passed the Spritsail barge Lady Daphne in full flow.

Off Southend Pier, we crossed the bow of the purposeful spritsail barge *Lady Daphne*. She was some distance off but she made a great camera shot. She was a grand sight indeed and to the west of the pier, the *Adieu* lay at anchor. Two spritsail barges: it was almost like days of old. Once we were heading into the Ray channel, we had to harden up appreciably. Some tacking was clearly likely for the crew to enjoy. It was a cracking sail up the narrowing low tide channel and sails were stowed as we neared my creek's entrance. What a way to finish…

Soon after berthing, my mooring neighbour, a chap known to us all since our childhoods, boarded his 100-year-old gaff cutter. Friendly words were exchanged as he got his boat ready to go out and we got ours stowed.

As we all took our leave of *Whimbrel*, we paused briefly to watch the departure of that pretty little ship, feeling more than smug with our own little cruise…

7
Milton Creek Revisited...

Having enjoyed a few days with two fellow boats of our class, *Calluna* and *Gypsy*, we enjoyed a glorious sail down from Chatham in company. We peeled away and left them outside Stangate Creek. They were bound for home. We, into the twisting run of Sharfleet Creek, a little gemstone within a cluster, to sit at anchor for the night.

The next morning, with a northerly and a somewhat cloudy sky, we sailed round from our Sharfleet anchorage, through the harbour at Queenborough and the Swale to anchor at Harty Ferry. We may have had a bit of a truncated sailing season during the first Covid spring of 2020 due to Covid-19 restrictions, but what sailing we were getting was of excellent quality, for sure.

During the afternoon, the sun broke through, lightening the day. We rowed ashore to the somewhat dilapidated hard on the Harty shore. Leaving the dinghy tethered to her anchor we set off for a walk. "Look at that sea lavender," I said as I tried to watch my footing too. The mate had already got a muddied foot!

"Yes, it's gorgeous…" I tried to capture its glory on my camera, but one can never do justice.

As we climbed to the level of the famous Ferry House Inn, the views are always well worth stopping to turn round and look at. While I was doing so, the mate walked across to look at a sign. It said 'closed'. We both thought that it would perhaps have been reopened. Sadly, not at the time, so no pint on the way back!

Whimbrel is never away from her home waters without a clutch of Ordinance Survey maps squeezed amid her bookshelf essentials. We'd agreed over breakfast that we would do this. So, fully armed, we took a route not taken before and left the road leading to the inn and the old ferry hard, cutting across the side of the hill eastwards towards Sayes Court and the old schoolhouse near the church.

It was a lovely little walk of not great duration but brimming with interest. The footpath was a haven of wildflowers and butterflies. Numerous bird types flitted about too, whilst above, skylarks serenaded us as we walked…

The church was closed, sadly, but it was as expected. It is a lovely place to sit and contemplate and it was definitely a year for that, surely. Passing the old schoolhouse after not seeing it for a few years was a bit of a 'shock' for it had been converted to a comfortable dwelling – a good use for what had become a ramshackle and dilapidated building. Up by the farm, chickens roamed the road. In fact, they were all over the place!

Back aboard, we settled for the evening in which the boat glowed, bathed as it was by a golden coppery sunset. For the first time on several occasions during the summer we had a quiet night in this anchorage. It is one of the best, but not in any wind-over-tide situation.

Waking the next morning we took the last of the flood west along the long run of the central Swale enjoying a sailor's breeze. For a short period, we butted the ebb, flowing east, but soon picked up where the tide split and took it westwards with us into the anchorage off Elmley Island, to the north, and a patch of saltings known as The Lillies, to the south.

The Lillies consists of a pool at the point where the tidal split returns towards the bottom of the ebb. It sits on the 'underside' of Elmley Island where Milton Creek's north/south run joins the Swale. There, an area of semi-fragmented saltings survives, bordering the pool and the eastern side of Milton Creek, the shaping, I believe, being indicative of the creek's ebb run being always northward. The patch is low and often submerged showing, perhaps, that siltation is slower than sea rise!

We had a plan. A walk on the wild side, round the wildlife lagoons below the village of Murston. The lagoons are waterfilled gravel and clay pits, once the domain of the brick and cement industry for which the creek was once king.

Having settled to our anchor and sitting with a coffee, we discussed the walk, I said, "…we need to be ashore about two hours before low water."

"Early lunch then…" I nodded, but we had an hour or so to make our own. The mate read for a while.

Checking my emails, I said, "Wow…"

"What?"

"The sailing barge *Dawn* is coming down from Queenborough later."

"What for?" the mate asked.

"Carrying cargo…for Milton…" I said, in a somewhat disbelieving manner.

"What about the bridge?" Yes, the bridge, across Milton Creek. It had headroom of just 4.5 m. It was enough to get the spritsail barge *Raybel* under with her gear laid flat on her deck. If only the bridge had an opening span, like those in Holland…it would have only been needed occasionally, on the tide.

"It's so sad," I say, "Would never have been allowed in The Netherlands!"

The local authority had renovated, and reopened Sittingbourne's Crown Quay situated at the head of Milton Creek. Upon it, the authority had built a replacement building for the Milton Creek Barge Museum, burnt down some years ago in dubious circumstances, at its old site at a derelict barge yard a little lower down-stream. An area of space was also being 'given over' for the care and repair of spritsail barges in an attempt to bring the sea back into this once busy port. Note my comments about the bridge – I have written strongly about this before!

The *Raybel* was due to go into a floating dock which had been the 'home' to the hull of the spritsail barge *Westmoreland*, a 'brickie' barge once owned by Eastwoods of Lower Halstow. The drydock had sunk, destroying the fragile barge within. Later in the year, the *Westmoreland's* broken remains were cut up. It was a sad end to a once pretty little spritsail barge. The *Raybel* was then floated in to begin restoration work.

My information said that the *Dawn* would off-load her small cargo into her barge boat for transhipment upstream. It was likely to be the first cargo taken into Sittingbourne by water for a very long time. At Queenborough that very afternoon, the cargo was being transhipped from a small sailing ship the *Gallant*, owned by the Blue Schooner Company. The Company had set up a trading route from the Caribbean, Portugal and ports along the English south coast to London and North Sea Continental ports.

Later, by the time of her expected appearance, I was hopping up and down, feeling quite excited: "We'll be unwitting witnesses…" I said, beaming at my mate, deeply enmeshed, reading her current novel.

The tide was dropping. I was looking at the tide tables, checking my going ashore calculations when my mate said, "Lunch now…" not as a question, but a statement. I nodded, affirming her query.

After clearing away our lunch things, we locked the hatches and left *Whimbrel* swinging on her anchor. Looking back, as we rowed ashore, she did look a picture. A bright splash of colour against the backdrop of the mudflats with their shell patches, dotted with waders poking for food. Amongst them were black-tailed godwits, I thought and avocet along the water edges waving their heads back and forth, skimming for food.

"Nearly there," Christobel murmured from her seat, aft, with a view ahead.

I swivelled my head, adjusted direction and moments later the dinghy's stem scrunched onto the hard-shell bottom. I poled her in further and stepped carefully out. "Hold on…I'll pull her in further." That done my mate carefully followed and I handed her ashore from the unsteady platform of the semi-grounded dinghy. She wandered off a little, looking about while I locked the oars to the thwarts!

The hard is very firm with a base of shell and stone. The latter predominates. Buried beneath are gas pipelines feeding the Isle of Sheppey. A little to the east is the largely intact hulk of a World War Two mine countermeasures vessel. She is listed over to port with her deck almost at mud level. The starboard side has, over the years, lost a large spread of her hull planking with it being exposed. Amazingly, one of a pair of davits still stands, as if awaiting the return of the ship's boat!

In the Swale wilderness, WW2 minesweepers slowly rot away.

Reaching the top of the hard, I gazed for a short time at the gnarled and largely broken up hull of another vessel. The structure fascinated me with its very heavy sectioned timbers. The little ships were crafted at a plethora of yards up muddy creeks outside the area of traditional shipyards to confound the 'enemy' of the time. After the conflict huge numbers were sold for firewood and reclaimed metals.

At the remembrance of firewood, I cast a furtive look across the water at *Whimbrel*, wondering briefly. It was the chilling thought about a threat made to burn her by a disgruntled local sailor after I'd asked 'yotties' to abide by the Covid laws then in force in a web blog. That was during the semi-freedom phase following the 2020 lockdown. It is covered later in the book.

Climbing the seawall, the mate looked at me inquisitively and asked, "Which way?"

Casting my thoughts aside for my good mate got fearful and upset, I said, "South, straight up the lane." Glancing at the map in my hand, before descending, we looked across a sea of scrub, water and a miscellany of dotted islands. The water had a deep green hue to it, indicating the presence of algae. Whether or not that affected its use as a bird reserve, I'm not qualified to say. In any case, it was the wrong time of the year. We were ashore for the walk and there was more to see!

The lane was a rough affair in places. My parents had dropped us off here many years ago after we had walked to Milton Regis to pay them a visit. They later dropped us back by car!

"Look…" Christobel said, grimacing. We had come across a pile of someone's unwanted belongings. There had clearly been an element of general rubbish dumping too. Madness! We knew the area had a superb recycling facility open to the public, having helped my mother empty herself of accumulated unwanted 'stuff' when moving from her Lower Halstow home.

Continuing our southward course, we passed a sanctuary, for what wasn't clear, then skirted a solar panel filled field. Other entrances made it clear they were little patches of privately owned land parcels, with dire warnings to keep out! Just before exiting onto a main road, the lane was diverted round a Travellers site.

"That was interesting," I said, grinning, adding, "not many views of the reserve…" We had passed access gates though and latterly, there were pools to both sides of the lane.

We crossed the road and threaded through modern infra-structure – a prodigious distribution warehouses – and came out by the village of Murston's old church. "Wow," I said, adding, "come on we must see this…" My mate, a keen historian in her way – being more interested in people – skipped after me.

Murston's old church regaining new life.

Years before, when the cement and brick industries were the area's industry, its vastness sucked at the old village's edges. The 'magnates' the Smeed Dean's owned it all. A look at any satellite view shows most of the area was once industrial – most still was, reincarnated as modern estates. Housing too had been built on some of the worked-out land, particularly away from the water where much of the heavy cement and brick firing was done. Old ordnance survey maps show the spread too and the route we were taking on our up-to-date copy. In fact, we have used a hundred-year-old map when walking further east, with perfect ease!

The tiny old church sat in its square of grass surrounded by a locally produced brick wall. The church, All Saints, originally had three chancels, built of flint and ragstone. It originally had a square tower and dated between 1375 and 1550. The footings of the original structure are buried to the north of the current chapel. It wasn't unusual for a church to be moved for the 'new' Victorian church was a half kilometre up the road. Big signs advertised a lottery grant for arts funding. The building was being brought back into use as a community arts centre, "The Murston HeArt Project" shouted one sign. By chance, we actually 'bumped into' the project's leader and chatted awhile, standing 'socially distanced' as was the need at the time!

From the church, we made our way towards Milton Creek and the Saxon Shore Way. At the creek was the well-preserved wharf last used by cement makers, Blue Circle. At its upper end, was a slipway, once used by the Smeed Dean barge yard. From the wharf, there was a short 'T' shaped pontoon into the creek. It was clearly disused. This place was once, for a short while, a base for the now-defunct Sittingbourne Yacht Club. The club had various homes, this, I understand, was its last. It being dislodged by the bridge.

One of the great plusses of the creek was its perfectly dished shape. This is probably due to areas of saltings bordering the creek which have not been reclaimed. It is only at its upper reaches where the creek rill begins to meander and the bed flattens as the water depth shallows. A brook does run in at the head from south of Sittingbourne. Around the creek's mud edges birdlife is fantastic. The close presence of modern light industry and man make no difference: it is the food rich mud they love. Autumn is the best time for birding types…

My mate was waiting for me, so breaking free of my reverie on the state of the creek and what had been lost, I reconnected and we proceeded downstream following the Saxon Shore Way. Well, we went off on our own route, passing in front of the old Brickmakers Arms, in use as a private dwelling and joining the 'way' below it. The map and direction signs were unclear…We had sailed up the creek some years ago, reaching the top near Crown Quay. The public house was then still open. We were chatting about it. "When was that?" the mate asked.

"Blimey," I said, "must have been ten years ago…" I wasn't far out either, looking it up much later!

Immediately below the bridge on the opposite bank sat Churchfield Wharf and a country park newly created from waste land running inland and downstream. It always feels eery walking under low road bridges with the thump of many tyres running over the expansion joints. We didn't linger. Further downstream we came across a pretty serviceable disused wharf. It and the Churchfield wharf could surely be brought back into use – the *Raybel* Barge Trust would be after a more convenient operational base at some point. *It's all ready for you guys*...I thought, chuckling stupidly!

Thorn scrub bordered both sides of the pathway at times, blotting any views. In places, large chunks of masonry and broken buildings lay jumbled along the inland side too. Reaching the area of what was known as the Marsh Berth, I'd dropped back by that point and my mate had gone on, obliviously. I knew a barge hulk was visible, having often spotted it from the water, so working my way through brambles, I found my goal. There before me, cocooned in cord grass to her deck level was the hull of the spritsail barge *Gladstone*. She was a little brick barge built in 1867 and was a mere 38 net tons. She was laid alongside the shore during the 1930's. Two of her sisters were built into the now decaying wharf, 'astern' of her, immediately downstream. The wharf was used to discharge London refuse for sorting. Burnable waste and ashes, including the unburnt coal dust, was used in the making of bricks. The mix produced a harder block, suited for higher-rise buildings.

Looking down Milton Creek over the entombed spritsail barge Gladstone.

I wandered the little barge's decks, wondering of her trading life in bricks and rubbish. Sadly, her end was the lot of so many of her sisters. Her poop deck and some of her aft cabin coamings were intact, as were her side decks running towards the mast waist deck. Her rigging irons stood ramrod, like a line of rust-red soldiers, devoid of their chocks on either side. Further forward, her hull was more broken. Her ragged and rotted stem and of her windlass bitts, just a single rotted spike poked from the mud and grasses. I was awoken by a call, "Where are you?"

"Coming," I yelled plaintively into the air like a curlew's call. Foolishly, I made my way over the old wharf. It was thick with low brambles and my legs beneath my shorts soon showed many bloodied scratches. I eventually made it back to the path, bubbling with laughter: the mate although still calling, didn't see me until I broke through. She didn't find it funny either!

"What were you doing…I lost you," my mate said, her lips puckering a little.

"I was alright," I said, hugging her gently. "I was looking at an old barge…"

Her look said it all, but she added, "Should have guessed!" The mate is fully aware that the creek is a repository of a plethora of barge hulks, most of which are buried in the saltings. Two other barges are visible, the *Nellie Parker's* fractured hull in the marshes adjacent to a carting track just below the site of the Dolphin Barge Yard, the other is the abandoned big steel barge *Celtic*, in the creek where the Dolphin Yard stood.

Going back to my earlier thoughts about a 'more useful' wharf to operate a spritsail barge from, it would be sad if more of the creek was not also brought back into use. I thought, if either Churchfields, fitted with a pontoon and gangway, or what was known as the Lower Berth could be made available, there could be a real heritage opportunity. Put bluntly, a barge could not keep having to lower and raise her gear to access a berth above the bridge every time she was taken out. Be madness!

Leaving the old wharf behind the path became a sea wall and our views were no longer hindered. It was clear that the tide was on the flood. Time for lingering was gone. All was well, as I looked out across the water towards our floating home too.

The last stretch had little of huge interest, apart from the expanse of the bird reserve and we were soon back at the top of the hard and strutting happily down towards the dinghy. The tide was almost back where we had left it a little over two hours earlier. We were soon away, rowing back to *Whimbrel*, ready for a pot of tea.

Later, while I was preparing our supper and enjoying a glass of beer gazing into the distance, to the north, I spotted the unmistakeable tanned triangle of the upper part of a barge's topsail. "Clear of the bridge," I murmured. It was always a heart-tugging sight, timeless and elemental. Very much part of the area's heritage. "The *Dawn*," I said, "she's coming …" The mate popped out to look too. It took the barge a little over 20 minutes to appear in her full glory from behind the Elmley hill and what a wonderous sight she was. As she came past a wharf, Grovehurst where gypsum is shipped in, her mainsail was being part brailed up. Her mizzen too. Passing in front of an angular multi-coloured works building ashore, *Dawn's* tan sails joined the patchwork of hues. Leaving those behind, she carried her way into the entrance to Milton Creek. There was still another two hours of flood, I reckoned, helping her. I stood watching as the barge shortened sail further whilst weathering a couple of bends past the Lillies saltings banks. Then, I saw her coming up into the wind near the position of the old rubbish wharf and her topsail dropped. She had clearly anchored. I was entranced, taken back to another age far less sophisticated than our own, more in the spirit of manana – tomorrow will do.

The spritsail barge Dawn, hull down below the saltings, slips into Milton Creek.

I was popping below, from time to time to 'stir the pot' and all the time I was grinning like a little boy who had just won a round of marbles. "Marvellous," I said, "marvellous," finally going below to give our meal preparation proper attention.

Unbeknownst to us, the *Dawn* passed us later in the evening, after dark, bound for Harty Ferry for a run up to Faversham. But sleep had overtaken *Whimbrel's* walk-wearied crew by then, so, sadly, didn't witness the last of this event…

8
Following an Old Waterway

It all began long ago; my dear mate was still teaching little children. It was also round the time I was 'dumped' from my career at sea – medically retired – literally beached!

"You need a break…" I said one morning, over breakfast.

"I can't…"

"Yes, you can…"

As is so often the case, a stray comment from my mate during a conversation with a friend brought to our attention the ancient town of Rye. It was a place we'd heard of, of course. I knew it was in East Sussex, but neither of us had visited.

In a moment of hopefulness, I began looking into weekend breaks round the area on internet web sites – the game was all new to me at the time! I found Rye. It had 'history' and looked enticing. Old, stuffed thickly with historic buildings and it had a waterway, but most of all I alighted upon a lovely looking family run hotel of relatively small size. The hotel overlooked the fishing harbour and the flatlands running away towards Kent, the write up gloriously enticed me. The delightful town of Rye sits just inside East Sussex with the River Rother's modern route running under its battlements. The short break was quickly booked.

Rye is one of two Ancient Towns in the group of Cinque Ports, created in medieval times to provide the King with ships for his navy. Winchelsea is the other. But Tenterden, deep inside Kent, remains a corporate limb of Rye, exposing it to interested persons and historians for sure as once a place attached to the sea.

I was both surprised and delighted to find that Rye had a busy yachting centre too. I soon found there were many boat yards and an active cruising section based at the Rye Harbour Sailing Club. The club's headquarters sits down at the seaward end of the Rother, but most cruisers berthed round the town's under-edge. The club dates to 1925 for cruiser yachts and a dinghy sailing club founded in1934. After amalgamation, the current name was incorporated.

A friend who sailed into the port during 'a bit of a blow' outside said he'd met a band of 'blokes' living aboard yachts berthed in the harbour. Some had begun with dreams of sailing off out into the blue yonder – the 'Med' even the Pacific – to faraway places. Some had 'lost' wives over the venture. Some had yet to make it down to the sea, preferring instead the 'gypsy life' afloat in a friendly old mud hole. Walking along the high harbour wall on one of our visits, I often wondered if some of those characters were still inhabiting the many live-aboard vessels I saw, many metres below my feet.

Section of c1710 map of Rye and Isle of Oxney area.

The fishing harbour, under the town's high old fortifications and the historic St Mary's Church, was an interesting start to a walk round the Rock Channel 'into' the old harbour where the town's other rivers meet the Rother.

The line of multi-coloured fishing vessels reeking of that heady quasi-saline-mollusc odour cast a spell upon me as I sauntered further than my mate to get a closer look. I'm not a fisherman but admire the tenacity of these coastal types who go out, whatever the weather, to return home, at times, with just the odd box to show for a day and half a night of hard graft.

We found the 'tarred' clapboard and rendered Ferry Cottage, sitting in its pretty garden. Leaning against an end wall were a long set of sweeps when we passed by, which made me chuckle a bit for they had a business-like look to them but were clearly underused. The cottage was seemingly far from the water of the Rock Channel – so called, presumably because it runs beside the rocky cliffs upon which the town stands. The ferry was reputed to have been run by just two families over the period of one hundred years. It was clearly a job to hold onto! The cottage once sat beside the stream, but the new channel was dug, apparently, to reduce flooding problems.

Under the rock cliff upon which Ypres Castle sits, I snuck down a lane from the ferry cottage to poke about a yard out on the flat nose of land formed where the rivers Brede and Rother meet. Incidentally, this was the site of the Rother Iron Works. It is also the lower end of the old harbour and the quays which then run up to its head, where a sluice for the Tillingham river issues into the harbour. The harbour channel was dug during other works, discussed later.

The old ferry cottage, Rye.

I just love wandering round these yards where one is bound to come across not one, but a mix of 'projects', some abandoned, whilst others not, but the history of small craft yachting abounds. Talking to a gnarled and weather worn yard owner years ago, I was told that as long as the rent is paid, the project stays…'Money for old rope,' I'd quipped, eliciting a wry smile from the old boy.

Returning to my mate, we wandered the road bordering the water, poking in here and there. The sight of a number of old fishing boats, hulls cut athwartships, upended and in use as sheds, was something seen elsewhere, but not in the numbers found. The 'quality' of some moorings would not have passed muster at my own yacht club, but it was difficult to see who had ownership of what. I deduced that much was privately owned and maintained for a narrow path led to many, outside yard bounds, as it were.

Typically, some waterfront buildings had been converted to cater for the holiday industry, sad, but often a practical means to maintain a small dwelling in use, rather than its destruction. Another turn took the harbour in a north/south axis past new developments. Opposite, immediately downstream of the River Brede's lock sat a yard visited during a walk mentioned later. From across the harbour, I saw that the boats were packed like sardines – so different to my own club's yard. However, on my visit, I felt an air of professionalism exuded.

The final leg of the harbour angled towards the sluice for the River Tillingham drain. We found the town-ward side of the harbour well-manicured with car parking off the busy road running alongside. The leg seemed to be where visitors moored, with long drops to decks with vertical ladders. My mate was aghast!

Boat owners seemed to prefer the opposite wall to moor and I could see why: out of 'reach' from 'prying sightseers' like us. Above the Tillingham sluice I saw a disused windmill, biding time as a bed and breakfast. The Tillingham river was explored no further.

Before we turned to go, my mate said, "Look at those drops," adding, "we're not coming here…" She was quite emphatic!

"Not much chance…" I said, laughing, as we turned towards the town's refreshment spots for a welcome coffee break…

A little-known fact is that Rye once had a ship building industry, but there again, many coastal towns did in some way or another. The River Rother spawned its own distinctive form of water transport for cargo and as likely or not for moving passengers too. There are no operational survivors except a vessel dug from the mud. She is called *Primrose* and her hull is on static display at The Hastings Shipwreck Museum. Why she was taken there, I cannot fathom: to my mind, she should have been kept at Rye!

Briefly, these vessels were developed for river work over many centuries, as was the much larger Thames Spritsail barge, but unlike the Thames type, the Rother barge was not designed to 'go to sea'…

The barge is thought to have been built in 1885 at William Clarke's shipyard which was sited off the Winchelsea Road, which means it must have been on the River Brede. She was unusual in that she had double-diagonal planking. She is said to be last of the wooden ones built. Steel was used for a number, latterly, when four were built by the Rother Iron Works at Rye. These vessels had a short mention by Frank G. G. Carr in his book, *Sailing Barges*, first published in 1931 and at various intervals since.

The vessels were around 17 m x 4.7 m with a small draft. They had an open hold aft of mast with a decked cabin forward. A gunter rigged sail was set on a mast positioned about at aft end of cabin, about a third length from stem. They carried approximately 20 to 30 tons of cargo, typically, but one at least was known to have carried 40 tons.

Interestingly, I visited Rye with my mate and her mother during September 1992, soon after the *Primrose* 'shivered' from her mud tomb and re-floated for her final water voyage down to the river's entrance where she was beached. The old ship was wrapped in tarpaulins. She had sat, wallowing in her entombment from around 1935, downstream of the town. I came across her near the sailing club. As was the case, even those many years past, I took a raft of pictures for posterity!

Looking up the old Winchilsea river.

Gradually, something about the place, the area, the waterway, seeped into me and I found a desire to explore more than just locally, rather than a mere tourist. It is only by really looking, walking an area and reading up about it that you can get an honest grasp. So, over time, a whimsy took hold of many of the outings we enjoyed as

I, well we, followed the old river, or tried to, both on foot and by car.

There was a 'memorable' local explore we made on by foot. The morning was drifting a little and in a wee spot of frustration, I'd said, "Come on darling…it's breakfast time…"

Christobel nodded barely breaking concentration in her doodling over a crossword, but a mouthed 'Okay…' signified an understanding.

'We need to get away on our walk promptly…' The spell was broken!

It was a gloriously hot day, Christobel had dressed in her 'best' summer frock, a swishy floral affair, with a pair of partial heels and looked delightfully ready for a luncheon date, rather than a walk… we went along like young lovers, hand in hand, chatting.

As the morning went on, we both discovered that 'the walk' was a WALK. I believe now that I'd measured the distance incorrectly, not for the last time either. I'm still reminded of this walk occasionally. Hey ho!

We followed the river, upstream, on the 'Kent' side. We crossed the entrance to a drainage channel to follow the Rother further inland until a footbridge was reached at a sluice and lock beside rocky cliffs, below Iden. We followed a lane and then a path indicated on our borrowed OS Map. At some scrub and thorn, my mate enquired, 'What, up there…'

"Erm, yes," I replied, bashfully pushing tentacles of bramble down, trampling them. As she stepped gingerly in my path, muttering a little, I cast back the comment, 'Nearly there…' It was answered by a welcome chuckle letting me know all was well. The path led us to Playden and the road back into Rye.

We arrived in town, hot and somewhat parched. We'd not taken any water. It was a long time ago and we're a lot wiser now. Amazingly, Christobel hadn't 'laddered her stockings' so it can't have been that bad!

But on another walkout to Winchelsea Castle and onto the outer harbour and back along Harbour Road, she, well both of us, went more suitably dressed.

Winchelsea Castle was built out on the flat land below the new town near the River Rother to protect the town from marauders, the French in the main. The castle is now known as Camber Castle. It was built in Henry VIII's time as a concentric artillery fort. It lies to the west of the river whilst on the waterway's eastern side Camber sands curls away into Kent, giving its name to the bay under the southern side of Romney Marsh.

When down near the sailing club enjoying some refreshments, I watched dinghies preparing to go off sailing, whilst others were returning with jubilant crews. The little boats with their multi-coloured sails flapping and snapping in the breeze, shivered and tugged in an effort to break free of their masters. My heart has always leapt at such sights when away, but time 'must' be spent doing other things. It was another long walk, but we'd better prepared ourselves. The road 'home' was found to be 'industrial', but people need to work to live – money doesn't grow on trees! Besides, the industry is a very necessary part of the landscape and often adds interest where none exists. I wasn't dissuaded from diving off on what are euphemistically called 'you're on your own explorations with detours into yards as the town was neared. The road virtually follows the route of a rail line that once served the outer or entrance harbour.

So, in the spirit of my old 'friends' Donald Maxwell, Herbert Thompkins and Walter Higgins and others; the ground-breaking Hoskins too, for I was looking at the landscape in more ways than one, I began to move beyond Rye. Before 'we' go, I must explain that I shall not become 'bogged down with history' for any reader can look this aspect up. My interest lies in the major changes and what I could see as I travelled as if I were sailing by.

The River Brede runs to Winchelsea and on, inland through flatlands up a rural valley. It was to Winchelsea, we went first. Old Winchelsea can no longer be visited for the environs of the original town were badly ravaged during storms in 1250 and 1252. Then in 1280s, part of the town was washed away in a violent storm.

By 1290 life became untenable and the town was abandoned to the sea and a new town laid out on its current hilltop position in a grid formation, seen in the old town today. A number of the original thirty-nine 'grid sections' remain empty to this day, they and other outlines clearly visible on a satellite view. The town is the town. Compared to Rye it is a haven of quiet without the multitudes of visitors that can, in effect, swamp a place. It was the 'below' I had a greater interest: New Winchelsea had a port too.

Of the port, nothing now exists. Along the River Brede, after the locks to Rye Harbour, there are a few boats to be seen, but in the main they are very small craft indeed. In effect, the river has lost its navigation too. Below the town, a stretch of the Military Canal runs along the foot of the hills to terminate close to the coast at Cliff End, to the south of Winchelsea.

The Tillingham river almost runs round the 'back' of Rye to join back with the Rother, but it cannot, due to the low ridge or causeway which runs out from Playden leading to the 'knoll' on which Rye stands. So, the river turns back on itself and worms inland up another valley to the north of Winchelsea's river.

These flatlands in the Rother Valley and off-shoots were once tidal, but through time the land level has risen and fallen, creating differing coastlines. Currently, apart from the slow sinkage of the southern half of Britain rotating on an axis, as a consequence of the last Ice Age, the fluctuations have apparently diminished towards a negligible number. 6000 years ago, nothing of what we call 'Romney Marsh' existed. Rye sat on the coast as did the eastern end of the Isle of Oxney and Appledore faced the sea.

Around 3000 years ago a combination of land rise and long-shore drift allowed marsh to form within what was a bay round to Hythe. The outline shape resembled rather like what we see now. It is thought that a watercourse ran out at Hythe and possibly, along a route similar to today's River Rother. The Romans 'enclosed' the northern part with a wall, thus 'preserving' it as the south became fragmented silt and marshy islands. The River Rother ran out to the sea south of the Roman 'inned' land at Old Romney. Over the next millennia, the outer shape of the Romney nose was created by siltation and inning of new lands. New Romney replaced the 'old' as the River Rother's seaport.

It was the same storms of the late 1200s that destroyed old Winchelsea that also became the death knell of the River Rother's exit to the sea at Old and then New Romney. The route of the river was changed 'permanently' with the creation of a shingle bar, cutting the harbour at New Romney from the sea. The coastline shift was of such magnitude that the river was forced to find a new route, so it turned somewhere near Appledore and ran south out past Rye's knoll.

Gradually, the long-shore drift of silt along the coast made the outer changes seen in today's Romney Marsh. With that problem, man, in his greed for new land, continued periodically to wall the salt marshes, thus reducing river flows, creating further land to be inned, until the status quo was reached of river runs and coastline we see today. Rye's fight with silt has been an ongoing saga for centuries and it was essentially written off by Admiralty Surveyors in 1698.

Interestingly, a new harbour was conceived around 1720 by Captain Perry. A harbour was built at a place now known as Winchelsea Beach, to the west of the Rother's current exit. Two stone piers projected out to sea with an entrance width of 200 feet. A channel or canal was dug from the harbour to the River Brede. A navigable sluice was set a little inland to control the level of water – an important point for shipping! The River Tillingham was diverted to feed the system and a new cut. It had been proposed that a cut was made to the north of Rye to feed the Rother into the new system too. In the event, the Rock Channel under the cliffs 'facing the sea' was altered, remaining in use to this day.

The project was completed, it is thought, by 1787, by which time Smeaton's name had been given to the harbour clearly due to his input to a straggling enterprise. Amazingly, the new harbour was in use for no more than three months. Problems with silting and land drainage caused a furore and it was simply abandoned. Wow!

Strangely, the changes to water flow round the town of Rye gave it back its harbour with a single channel to the sea, whereas before there were two. And, beyond the little hotel, we had grown to love, out over the flats south of where I gazed on a balmy evening with a dram, lost courses are faintly discernible on modern satellite mapping.

West of a nature reserve in a place known as Winchelsea Beach you can find Smeatons Lane. It leads down past a wide swathe of grass – probably the old harbour site – to the sea. Maps of the 1870 period show this area as an infilled section of land. Inland from the green is a large pool of water with a 'creek' running inland in line with a trackway, named 'Old River Way' terminating close to the banks of the River Brede, in a line toward Rye. I have no proof but believe this to be the course of the 1700s' channel. Following storms in 1967, wooden stakes forming the foundations of the piers reappeared after a beach shift. At the time it was a news event, locally.

Today, Rye Harbour Sewer runs across the Pett Level, draining the low land into the River Rother, downstream of Rye's harbour.

So, we went exploring, by car, as my 'friend' Donald Maxwell had done one hundred years previously.

Jill Eddison, in a paper, *Developments in the Lower Rother Valleys up to 1600*, discusses two major course changes of the River Rother in historic times. Various old maps can be pulled up online covering the area. Prints too are available, purporting to be 'originals' – Yes, right! Copies, more likely…

In Saxon times, the river flowed through the Wittersham Levels south of the Isle of Oxney. During the fourteenth century the river was diverted with a dam. That was except for a small flow along the old route, along the top of Oxney, past a little place called Smallhythe and on to 'beneath' Appledore, once a port itself. The dam was called the Knelle Dam, otherwise known as the Bush Dam – a name found on current ordnance survey maps. What volume of flow was allowed down across the Wittersham Level through some form of sluice is unknown. Here may have been the inadvertent 'mistake' of the project. Knowledge of levels, sluices, pumping and know-how over the last two hundred years far surpasses what our forefathers knew and understood. Mistakes happened.

The Appledore 'spur' – was the harbour sited behind it?

It was dammed in a bid to control tidal swamping inland along with an excess of fluvial flows. However, routing the river 'northbound' created further problems. Along with this, the River Rother's flow out across Romney Marsh was terminated in the same storms of 1287 which destroyed old Winchelsea. The river 'burst' through southward, leaving Appledore 'high and dry' and joined the smaller 'Rye' rivers in their seaward flow, giving Rye water for its harbour. Historians believe the Rother's flow had already split as early as the 1250s, with some going east past the 'Romneys' and some south, under Rye's nose. There is a view that the northern route remained 'in use' towards the dawn of 1700. But the Knelle Dam is recorded as being breached 'in 1600 or thereabouts' to send the Rother back down its old route, effectively reducing the northern route to a ditch. There is far more to this subject, including land levels, shrinkage from underlaying peat drying and fascinating as it may be, I leave it to you, reader, to investigate further at your leisure…

From Rye, the Rother runs northwards past the hills of Playden where it briefly joins the grand Military Canal. The canal was built between 1804 and 1809 and runs from Hythe to Rye and then across the Pett level to Cliffe End. The waterway was abandoned in 1877. Leaving the canal, the river turns west to wind along the underside of the Isle of Oxney. On 'bottom corner' of the Isle, a familiar name crops up. It is one found in more than one place round the Thames Estuary – Coldharbour. It is affixed to a cottage, but more likely to have been a place or farm, although the name doesn't appear on mid-1800s' maps.

We drove to Appledore and played at being tourists, enjoying a mid-morning coffee. The village sits on a bluff with a hooked nose, behind which, surely, a harbour once sat. Just before reaching Appledore, there is a sluice, the Reading Sewer, which runs west over the top of the Isle of Oxney to the old port of Smallhythe, the lost port for the Wealden town of Tenterden, in the heart of the Kent.

The ground is high at Appledore and the cliff's drop to the road alongside the military canal. The sandstone cliffs run northward at varying heights, on to Hythe in Kent – forming what was once an ancient coastline. South of the old town and harbour is Snargate, the first of a string of towns along the course of the waterway to the sea.

The waterway was bounded by what was called the Rhee Wall. It separated Romney Marsh proper and Wallend Marsh – the area to south to Camber Bay. It ran in a generally easterly direction away from Appledore before curving south-east to Snargate and Breznet, turning easterly to Old Romney and onto New Romney. Two roads, the modern-day B2080 and the A259 follow the route today. I have read that the wall was built by the Saxons from Appledore to Rye. That may have been so for it would predate the later actual wall by some 400 years or so. Rhee, means, a watercourse. So, a 'water course wall' now more commonly known as a sea wall or riverbank…

The wall had two embankments with a raised level between them. The River Rother lay outside and was essentially the waterway's last route across Romney Marsh. But and there is always a 'but', the waterway was pushed south by inning, deeper into Guildeford Marsh, east of Rye (now a named E. Sussex district). It was also forced to turn sharply north by the inning inside the Lydd nose, where an island had become established over the centuries. Clearly, man and nature were in combat.

The walls and waterway with sluices at Snargate, Breznet and Old Romney, was built in thirteenth century to try and control the siltation of the River Rother. In 1258 – that date again – it was extended to New Romney. However, as we already know, in 1287, nature had other ideas and New Romney was severed from the sea! We followed the route, looking, but there is little to see, except for the New Sewer which weaves a route from Snargate, through Breznet, passing near Old Romney to run out over the beach, just north of New Romney. The last of the old waterway, surely.

What must be remembered is that this waterway was once of huge significance. In a delightful book by Ronald and Frank Jessup, *The Cinque Ports*, they do not give a date for the establishment of the Cinque Ports for it is unknown, but some form existed in Anglo-Saxon times. The grouping may have been existence prior to 1066, but by the next century a pattern of specially licensed ports was well established – 1155 by Royal Charter. Interestingly, Rye was a limb of New Romney, but after the storms of 1287 caused the River Rother to change course, Rye became an 'Ancient' of the ports. New Romney remains a Cinque Port, Lydd as a limb, with other marsh 'ports' as non-corporate members.

Standing at the edge of the road by the Reading Sewer, under Appledore, I imagined a harbour with carracks berthed at a Hythe. The hustle and bustle of cargo being moved about. The evocative smell of spices from afar. Shipmasters arguing the toss about little or nothing…wharfingers shouting to be heard…the town's traders vying to sell stores to a ship readying to depart…sailors promising their 'ladies of the night' they'd soon return, blowing kisses as they ran hurriedly up gangplanks…Yes, it was all in the breeze, ruffling my ears and caressing my cheeks.

My reverie was broken by a 'come on…I'm still here…'

The Kent boundary largely runs along the River Rother to south of the Isle of Oxney and far inland. However, for a short period, many centuries ago, Sussex got hold of Oxney, but it is said the people rebelled and Oxney was returned to Kent. As a Man of Kent, that's as it should be!

Taking the road inland from Appledore and looking down on the chequered verdant fields and sea of green pastures, I stopped the car (we were holidaying with my open topped MG 160TF), looking, I said, "It is difficult…" pausing before adding, "to envisage a wide busy tidal river down there." My mate nodded, her mind more on the glorious scenery that surrounded us.

The road dropped down onto the flat land. Crossing the Reading Sewer, we stopped by the Ferry Inn – Isle of Oxney Inn – and I went for a snoop. The water flowed languidly beneath its banks past this ancient crossing onto Oxney. I was surprised at how wide it looked – enough for a little motor cruiser, certainly, perhaps a sailing dinghy? Doubtful!

The Inn was built it is said in 1690 when the River Rother was up to a quarter of a mile wide in places. Upstream, sits the Isle of Ebony or Chapel bank, one of at least two islands along the Rother's northly course. The ferry was once a busy place for crossing points were few and far between.

We crossed onto the island, passed through Stone village, stopping by the ancient church of St Mary the Virgin, which has an ancient Roman stone altar within. Below the church, a little divorced from its village was Coldharbour. Our path threadled through the heart of Oxney, passing down the centre of Wittersham, the village that gives its name to the levels round Oxney, although various names abound. Before dropping down at the western end of the island, where the road runs for a short way on the old Bush Wall, there are views west up the Rother valley and the valley between Tenterden and Rolvenden.

The weald of Kent and East Sussex was a major centre of iron smelting and overgrown pits and works can still be found scattered here and there. W. G. Hoskins says that the industry had steadily changed the landscape by the sixteenth century. Here he meant, a denudation of trees used for the iron making process, opened up the land. The River Rother would surely have been one of the main export routes from the locale.

Smallhithe House above the old quay fronting it.

We enjoyed an excursion to Tenterden before dropping back to Smallhythe.

We'd visited Tenterden many times over the years since finding Rye: it is a delightful Wealden town with a wide main street lined with ancient in use buildings.

The house originally known as the Port House, dates from when Smallhythe was a port. It was apparently built around the end fifteenth century. It is currently cared for by the National Trust. The Victorian actress Ellen Terry lived there from 1899 to 1928 and it was a collection of her theatre attire that specifically interested my mate. Me, I just wanted the outside, which was where I headed first! I wanted to soak it in, get a feel…

Walking across the garden, which drops away down towards the Reading Sewer, I imagined the Hythe, busy with craft. Earlier versions of the Rye barge, perhaps, medieval open craft carrying a few tons. A tang of salt, in from the estuary, tainting the Wealden fruit-scented air.

It wasn't like that. Beyond, was a sea of green farmland. The waterfilled ditch gave me no hints. Without prior knowledge, more than an imagination would surely be needed. There is nothing to suggest a seafaring connection! The 'Time Team' an archaeologist investigative television programme filmed a dig here, I seem to remember. The team came up with wharf remains, nails and roves from ship repair operations.

"Come on…" I said, meeting my mate back in the house, "I'm done. Nothing much here…typical of its type…" glancing back at the small display depicting its maritime connections.

"I enjoyed it," she quipped. Yes, she did. We left the National Trust to preserve its bit of history.

From Smallhythe, the Reading Sewer snakes southward round the western end of Oxney where it drains into the Newmill stream. At the Potmans Heath Pumping Station, the combined flows head seaward at a sluice at the Bush Wall. The sluice runs under the Wittersham/Maytham Road. The Newmills stream flows down a shallow valley west of Tenterden.

Stopping at the sluice, I gazed down the stream towards the sea. All was languid and tranquil. Where ever I looked, none of the area's history could be detected, nor the once extensive brickworks and wharves.

To go west, one must go north or south for the river's flatlands remain devoid of modern transport routes, apart from the privately run rail line of the Kent and East Sussex steam railway. The line was closed in the 1960s by the infamous Dr Beeching. Public footpaths are similarly scarce. The river remains, to this day, the only direct east/west passage!

We travelled inland as far as Newendon Bridge having to make a journey inland towards Rolvedon first. At the bridge, I looked down at the Bodiam Boating Station, a busy hive for river cruising on the River Rother. The river looks 'man-made' and semi-sterile. This was especially so, upstream, where, with a number of bends, it travelled west with treeless banks, through the flat landscape.

Off the Newendon to Rye Road, a lane leads north to Great Knelle, where there is a group of cottages. The lane winds down to the River Rother, close by a pumping station. This is the western point of the Knelle Dam (Bush Wall). According to mid-1800s' OS

Maps, a Brick and Tile works operated from the river's south bank, on the edge of higher ground, beneath Brickhurst Wood.

The River Rother near Bodiam boating station.

Maps of the 1800s clearly show brick and lime manufacturing with associated wharves dotted along the river networks in both Kent and East Sussex. One works at Maytham Wharf, became divorced from the course of the Rother possibly after its rerouting again, although the Hexden Channel runs past it now. The wharf lies immediately inland of the infamous Bush or Knelle Wall.

By looking at sites, such as Google Earth, the unmistakeable lines of cuttings, tram lines and such in green fields bordering the river can be seen in places, especially I believe, either side of Knelle, where, as has been said, a works existed on south side of the river.

Looking at old maps, sheepfolds – protective 'islands' – abound all-round the Isle of Oxney and the levels, just as they once did in the low land areas and marshes of my beloved east coast waters. It is so easy to forget how tidal this land was. But for sea defences, it would surely become saltmarsh again, something that is a likely probability one day, however hard man tries.

From the 'sea lock' upstream of Rye, there are no further locks on the river's run through its surrounding pastureland. The land rise is minimal. But for the sea defence nature of the sluice at this spot, the land would flood. Essentially, the river is maintained with a continuous drainage run to the sea and any fluvial excess when the tide is too high is controlled by pumping.

It is a fact that many of the old ports which were once so important they were made Cinque Ports in own right by Royal Charter, or were a limb, with a flourishing trade and financial ability to own ships, had now receded into obscurity, far from their sea connections.

So, we will leave the river, which had such a large share of medieval importance and trade, snaking into the wilds of the Kent and East Sussex borderlands.

Would I eventually sail into the Port of Rye one day? Highly doubtful, but we enjoyed 'sailing' the river and its ancient streams on our land exploration.

9
Morning Mishap on the Alde

We were walking back from a rather pleasant pub on the northern side of Snape Bridge. There was an element of bonhomie amongst the group: some good ale had accompanied our delightful meal.

Stopping, to pause for a look over the bridge's parapet, I gazed at the reflections of buildings on the remaining run of water in the creek. The rest had stopped too, I looked at them and I said, quietly, as if not to disturb anyone else, 'Remember, it's an early start in the morning…'

One chuckled, mentioning a nightcap. My sister said, 'Yes, you said earlier…' From the other, no comment other than an audible sigh!

Before continuing to walk, I turned to gaze down the creek, up which the tide would appear in not so many hours. The oozy mud glistened back to reeds growing profusely along the northern bank. I knew that when the tide reached into them, we would be away.

The previous day, with my crew, which consisted of my sister, Theresa and friends, Hannah and Steve, we'd sailed up from Aldeburgh from a mooring off Slaughden Quay. I'd encouraged my crew to sail it, as best they could, with limited use of the engine and without the use of my then-new toy, a GPS map unit. They made it to just below the quay at Snape. The wind was a friendly south-easterly, which helped them immensely. I was proud of them! Hannah had acted as chief lookout. The numerous withies since the two 'Troublesome Reaches' down under Iken Church were passed by, appeared erratic at times. It was a job well done.

Upon mooring, we'd all had a walk round looking at the trappings of tourism as well as the old malting buildings. From various rooms of the famous hall converted for concerts – in honour of Benjamin Britten, who had lived locally – the sounds of instruments could be heard. Perhaps preparations for an evening performance, whatever, it was a nice touch!

Round the grounds there were works of art to be found, in the form of sculptures, which children naturally found fun to play upon – probably the whole point! After tea and washes, one by one as others nattered, read, or just watched the world go by, the boat's water supply was topped up in readiness for our morning departure.

Whimbrel alongside at Snape.

Over a beer and nibbles, we talked through the next day, with a planned early departure and eventual stop-over at Orford. My sister had been the old port before, but the other two crew hadn't. It was also a convenient jumping off point for Harwich, a particular request of my crew for I'd pumped them up about the historic town.

At the mention of thinking about a departure time, Hannah groaned. Steve laughed, murmuring something in Welsh. Here, I should add, Steve claims to be Welsh, but when pushed, yes, he was brought up in Wales – Isle of Anglesey actually – he is in fact only a quarter Welsh, being the most part from middle Europe! But let Steve be Welsh: it is good for his soul!

My sister said, "You can stay in bed…" looking coyly at the other girl and smiling knowingly.

I grinned, for I knew from many early starts that the poor girl was not good in the mornings. It was something I'd learnt years before when just the girls had enjoyed the best part of a week aboard. It was during that trip that I learnt that Hannah's husband had sailed in his younger days and his brother kept a boat in the Anglesey area. On Hannah's first sail aboard *Whimbrel*, I'd got her on the helm soon after leaving Titchmarsh Marina, comfortably going down the Walton Channel and left her to go forward to help my sister hoist the main. It was then I learnt, in a whispered conversation, that Hannah hadn't helmed a boat since leaving university many years earlier. By heck, there wasn't a problem though…she was like a pro! My sister, on the other hand, is very well qualified, technically and practically and has been sailing with me aboard *Whimbrel*, or with the mate and I for years.

"No," Hannah said, grimacing a little, "I'll get up…" then, smiling thinly, she muttered something along the lines of "I'll make the tea…" No time had yet been mentioned, but they all knew what time we'd arrived and that tides move in unstoppable cycles!

"Okay," I said, "We need to depart a little after daylight, say at five…" All had nodded. "Cheers then, it was a good day…" so, lifting my glass of beer, draining and savouring those last drops, I added, "Let's go and find our supper…"

The alarm, in the early hours can be an awful thing. Drugged with sleep after a previous busy day, one's senses are assaulted with a seemingly unstoppable piercing shrill, young-girl-like scream. I reached up to a shelf and shut it off. On the bunk opposite, my sister's eyes opened.

Swinging my legs out and pulling on my shirt, I heard from the main cabin a Welsh-like grunt with a mumbled, 'I'm awake…' Grabbing my shorts, I finished dressing and 'hopped' up through the fore hatch, leaving the cabin to my sibling. It was twenty to five.

Outside, it was a glorious late July morning. It was quiet. There was no discernible breeze under the eaves of the malting's buildings. The morning colours ran out into a deep blue above the boat. I was getting the last of the two springs off after reducing fenders and letting the dinghy off onto its painter alone when the hatch slid back and the cheery grinning face of shipmate Steve said 'tea', handing me a mug.

My sister appeared and then, lo and behold, the last of the waking faces grinned out from the companionway. Steve chuckled, as I laughed: it has happened virtually every time Hannah has sailed aboard *Whimbrel*, with at least one early start to contend with. This trip there were two! It was just before five…

"Okay, let's get going…" My sister went forward to tend to forward breast rope and I gave the stern line to another. Moments later we were away, under power, puttering over a tide that was about full.

It was almost mesmerising passing through the banks of reeds so close by whilst we, in deep water, swished by, the engine just above tick-over. The water was coated with reflections ahead and as we passed 'through them' they were broken then rippled and left to reappear in our wake, ripples lessening until order was restored.

After a bit of a squiggle in our course, the banks curved round through the easts until on a southerly route. Past a bit of a point, a u-bend was followed. It was going swimmingly well.

"That way…" a voice said.

"Port or Starboard…" I said, quietly, looking at a weedy withie quivering close by. I noticed that the tide seemed to be on the ebb.

"Port," the same voice immediately retorted. I steered a little to port. We were by then coming out of the big 'U'…for some reason, I had a judgement flutter with a deep feeling of 'I don't like this…' The bank seemed far to close on the starboard side, yet, lit by the sun's rays beaming in from the east the creek looked deep in the light cast across the water, into the saltings and on a bank of trees.

"Too far to starboard…" I heard.

Whimbrel slowed, clearly feeling the bottom. I could see a withie ahead. We seemed to have the line. "Port…" a voice said.

I got the boat moving again and stupidly thought, *Blimey that was close*…and promptly ploughed to another halt. No matter what I did, *Whimbrel* was fast. The tide was clearly dropping too.

The illusion of deep water had fooled me, I could see that all too quickly, but far too late. A beacon was in line ahead of us, but something else was wrong…

We had been underway for just 25 minutes.

I was quickly declining into a mood of complete despair. My crew made drinks and kept quiet while I studied and studied again the tide tables, aware of what the figures meant. The tides were falling into a period of neaps. I had visions of poor *Whimbrel* being upon this bank, for it was abundantly clear that I had managed to perch us right on the edge of some flats edging the saltings running across to Iken Wood. Ahead, through the boat's stationary bow, the houses grouped along Iken Cliff were in full view. I could see a couple of people, talking and pointing our way.

All I could see was for me to dump the crew ashore, later, at a landing by those houses and having to call my good mate and ask her to drive up and collect the crew…

I couldn't see a way out!

I sipped my tea. As the tide fell further, I could see where I got on, then essentially off, to go back on again. The stern was on the downward side of the lip of the mud flat. A thought occurred to me, *Dig her out*. My father had to do that during 1949 in Benfleet Creek. He'd put his father's boat into the saltings on the Canvey Island shore, just west of the train station on the mainland.

"Let's have breakfast…" the girls intoned, almost in unison.

"Good idea…" piped Steve, adding, "I'm hungry…" I felt afterwards that this had been a set-piece, to dig me out of my melancholy.

"Right," I said, smiling thinly, "then we'll discuss the what-ifs…" I looked round, it was, dare I say it, sublime. The early morning's promise of a calm sunlit day was all about us. Below, was all busyness as the two girls set to over breakfast preparations.

"Fruit…" a voice said, passing plates and other items out into the cockpit. Fruit has always been available aboard *Whimbrel*, I usually say, "you'll not catch scurvy on my ship…"

Soon, plates of egg, bacon, mushrooms and tomatoes were being passed out. Toast to follow, one of the girls said, exiting from below. It was a good breakfast. It restored my despondent heart greatly. I knew what I, we, needed to do, but would the other man in my crew want this.

"So," Steve began to say, licking the marmalade spoon, "what do we need to do?"

It was a direct question. It needed a direct and honest answer,

"Well," I said, "if we can dig some mud away, I am sure we'll get off when tide returns…"

"Okay."

"There aren't any shovels," I quickly said, adding, "we've two bowls and a bucket in the locker…"

"Right, let's get to it!"

"Let your breakfast go down first…" one of the girls said, firmly.

"Have you told the mate yet?" my sister asked, grinning a little. I shook my head. "Shall I do it?" she added. It was a bit of a copout, but I acquiesced.

After a little while, I looked at Steve and he looked at me. "Come on," he said, a grin as wide as could be. I got up reached into the poop locker and pulled out the dip bucket, removing its lanyard. I also pulled out the cleaning bowl. These were dropped into the dinghy which I had earlier put alongside to port.

We shucked down to our underpants. I had some swimmers with me, but pants would be easier to wash!

Saying, "Okay…" I led the way along the side deck. I felt *Whimbrel* wobble a bit, but she was sitting in mud after all!

Stepping into the mud from the dinghy's transom was a 'funny' as my legs slid deeply below the surface. It felt cold down there to my toes! I looked under *Whimbrel's* bottom. The long keel had not completely sunk in, but she's clearly settled.

"What we need to do is move mud to create a bit of a channel," I said, adding, "if the stern floats, she'll come off…"

Steve dived under the bottom and began 'shovelling' mud while I shovelled what he moved further away, sending it skidding down the creek bank. It wasn't long before we were both plastered…

"Called the mate," my sister called down, "she said you're a silly idiot…and to keep her posted." I think perhaps that was a heavily diluted transcript of their conversation!

We dug and dug. In what seemed a short space of time, was very nearly an hour. We'd made quite a dent in the bank.

I became aware of voices above, quiet ones, whisperings, but couldn't see. Then, sniggering and light laughs drifted down where I was up to my nether regions digging away round the aft end of *Whimbrel's* keel. Looking up, I found myself staring straight into

the lens of a camera being moved about. "Steve, they're filming…"
I exclaimed! A guffaw floated through his legs along with another
load of mud.

Soon after we had got into it, I found that the bowl I had, was
of more use as a support when moving and bare hands formed into
a scoop moved more mud. The other thing I found was that a little
below the surface, it was obvious that the edge we were on was once
the edge of saltings. Rotted roots were in the mix.

"Coffee and biscuits…" called a voice from above. Looking up,
my sister, with a huge grin, was looking down at me. In one hand
she clutched two mugs. I wiped a hand as best I could. Mugs and
biscuits were passed. "You're doing well," she said.

Digging her out … thanks Theresa Ardley! Author's collection.

Refreshed, we were soon hard at it again. The dip in the creek's
bank got ever bigger. My crewmate, worked wonders, reaching in as
far as he could, burrowing vole-like.

"Look," a voice from above called, "the withie you missed is
over there…" It was my sister, bless her.

"Pity you didn't say earlier," I called, tongue in cheek.

The quick retort came, as I knew it would, "It was underwater then…"

'Ha-ha!' Beyond, was a broken off post with weed swinging provocatively, as if taunting me…

We dug on. I moved Steve's mud in between moving more away from round the rudder and aft keel area.

Above, the two chattering female voices suddenly stopped. Then an exclamation about something or other. Then a voice called loudly, "Boat's moved…"

"What?"

"*Whimbrel* moved just then," my sister said, looking down at me.

My crew was well under the port bottom pulling glutinous mud out, "Out Steve, now," I said firmly.

He turned and 'swam' himself some way out, losing off an expletive in Welsh, 'Diawl uffern…', before grinning madly. It didn't need a lot of translation, but sounded like 'Bloody hell…' Later he explained, diawl, means devil and uffern, means hell. Pretty close then!

I was under the quarter, so, looking round the other side of the rudder, sure enough, the unmistakeable sign of a slippage was clear to me. 'Is the tiller free?' I called, looking up towards an invisible head.

'Is now,' a voice intoned, moments later. And my sister's head appeared over the transom.

"Definitely moved," I said, looking at Steve, "be careful from now on, think we'll have a break…" looking back towards two female faces finding life highly amusing.

After a further mug of tea, we dug on. By excavating along the underside of the keel, I could feel the boat slipping gently downwards. At intervals, comments from above confirmed this. One of the girls climbed down into the dinghy waving a camera about. Amazingly, none were taken on my own camera!

The morning moved on too and the sun beat down, but a breeze was coming from the southwest curling round the boat's hull and cooling us. I felt that a good stiff breeze was likely by the evening.

Eventually, I looked at what we had achieved from a distance away from the boat to get a better picture. I called to Steve, "I think we've done enough…" I felt confident of *Whimbrel* re-floating on the incoming tide, which I had seen was running in up the creek, a little while before. Steve, his infectious grin still in place, nodded, mumbling in his native tongue.

By the time we had finished burrowing, crab-like, beneath *Whimbrel's* now muddied bottom and round her keel from midships, running back to the rudder, the boat had dropped some forty centimetres in height aft. She'd slid backwards down the bank by nearly a metre too, it seemed. Unlikely as it was, she seemed all set for a toboggan ride!

Calling up to my sister, I asked if she could dig out the kedge from its stowage beneath the cockpit sole boards. Also, a long warp to be found in with the other mooring warps. I ran the anchor out down into the creek in a downstream position. I reckoned that as soon as the boat picked up, the tide's pull would automatically pluck *Whimbrel* off.

Steve followed me down into the stream. It was warm. We swam round, letting the dried and glutinous lumps wash away. I carried a bucket of water up to the dinghy to enable us to clean our legs, after a fashion. Handing up the cleaned bowls, my sister, bless her, got the necessary together for us to have a freshwater wash down on the foredeck. My 'wonder man' had first turn.

In a short while, we were tolerably clean. The new plan was to stop at Aldeburgh and make use of the club showers there, so clean was relative. I looked at my pants – yuck! I wasn't sure how much washing was going to be needed to make them fit for purpose again…we both decided the bin was best!

'Some lunch boys,' sang out of the main cabin hatchway and both Steve and I rubbed our fronts in anticipation. During the meal, we all watched the tide running fast up the ever-widening channel and creeping inexorably up the bank towards where our 'big hole' was.

Once the tide had reached the dinghy I got down and cleaned out muddied patches and swished *Whimbrel's* sides too, watching as the tide crept up the boat's rudder. Finishing and climbing back aboard, I said, "Should we have some tea now?" indicating where the tide had reached.

No sooner than we'd finished that tea and with the pot replenished, *Whimbrel* shivered a little. "She'll pick up soon…" I said, adding, "when she does, things will move fast…" I explained that the stern line taken forward earlier and run outside everything would act as a bow mooring as she swung to the tide. I would cast it off aft…in the event, it went like clockwork.

During the mid-afternoon, *Whimbrel* picked up and slid free of the bank. The mooring was let go aft and moments later *Whimbrel* lay to her anchor, her bow pointing downstream to 'the sea'…

It was an uneventful run back downriver to Aldeburgh. Passing the cottages at Iken Cliff, several people watching from their gardens which run down to the water's edge, waved. Someone called out, "Well done…" or something like it! An hour and a half later we picked up one of the visitor buoys off the Martello Tower. The club's launch ranged alongside and offered to take us ashore with the dinghy in tow. He waited while towels were grabbed…

Getting back aboard from the dinghy was highly dangerous indeed. I accomplished our crew transfer in two trips: a blustery wind over tide situation had developed in the north-south run of the Alde, as it does often here. It was atrocious, dangerous even, in the short waves and sluicing tide.

The club's boat had shut down for the night, so with no one to ask, I said, without any compunction, "Let's get out of here," and started the engine. The girls were below making supper preparations. 'Stow everything safely, I added. The bow was beginning to plunge so having instructed my sister to take care and clip her harness onto the safety line, she cast us off. I motored round the corner a little past the old quay at Slaughden and picked up a vacant buoy near some other visiting yachts.

Out of that horrid wind over tide situation, were found the evening was quite serene and Steve and I were given a beer to keep us occupied while supper was prepared. We toasted our success, with cheers all round. Most importantly, I toasted my superb crewman who did the unexpected…a fine shipmate.

Enjoying our supper with a rather nice glass of wine from a bottle brought aboard by Steve, I said, "You know," looking more towards my sister, "I shall never know why I didn't use the GPS on the way up…" she nodded, smiling as if knowing this already, knowing too the final point I quickly made, "…I'd have known the route!"

Then, in unison, they all burst into laughter, the girls saying, "Cheers…" and Steve, "…iechyd da." (Good health).

Postscript: the following year, the same group joined the ship at *Whimbrel's* home berth, staying overnight at our home before our departure. Over our dinner, Steve, to great hilarity, was presented with a child's plastic beach bucket and spade. He has kept them as a memento. Bless!

10
Barging on the Blackwater

My first memory of 'barging on the Blackwater' was a very long time ago. It took place towards the end of 1964 aboard the spritsail barge *May Flower*, which was my childhood home.

Following a collision with another barge off Southend in June of that year and needing repairs, the *May Flower* was towed from the River Medway to Maldon for the work to be carried out by Cook's Barge Yard as soon as the school holidays started. It was virtually the last job by the firm before the yard changed hands. The story is told about in my first book, *The May Flower a Barging Childhood*. A memorable sail took place over Boxing Day and the following day of that year, during our passage back to our home berth in Whitewall Creek on the River Medway. I remember it being exceedingly cold, but the weather was sublime. The crew kept a pot of tea hot on the fo'c'sle stove and being given sips with lots of rum in – I was nine and a half…

It was to be nearly 40 years later that I had another barge trip on the River Blackwater – A real hands-on event. It took place aboard the fine steel barge *Wyvenhoe*, then owned by a sailing friend. We joined the barge for a weekend over my birthday with a couple of the owner's crewing friends, sailing away from Maldon in the early morning darkness. By the end of the day, we'd sailed up the River Colne where we moored overnight at the delightful waterside town of Wivenhoe. During the passage back to Maldon – it would have been a Sunday – I found to my surprise that I was left at the wheel, tacking upriver towards Osea Island. The skipper said, "I need to go below…" On his return, he left me to it…we caught up with the 'mighty' *Reminder*, but she stowed sail and motored ahead of us with her weekend passengers. It was a cracking finale to a good day's sailing.

More recently, during the autumn of 2020, I had the opportunity with Christobel to join the Sea-Change Sailing Trust's fine new vessel, *Blue Mermaid*, for a day afloat. It fitted into a 'relaxed' period of the year's Covid-19 rules and regulations that were then governing our lives. On deck, 'distancing' was achieved as best one could on a working vessel. Below, distancing and the wearing of masks was expected. Whilst hauling on a halyard later, can't remember what, I famously chirruped, 'No kissing…' which immediately caused great mirth round the mainmast foot…

We arrived at our joining point at Heybridge on the River Blackwater before there was any sign of the new dawn showing down river, away to the east. It was late October and dark! It was a gorgeous morning though with a soft south-westerly breeze, a little overcast, but the night cloud was breaking nicely. Round us, in the morning's quiet, waders and gulls were waking from their roosting places and beginning to squabble for food sources.

Stupidly, I initially took us to the wrong yard, but hearing voices, realised before a crisis developed. Then I suddenly remembered the specific instruction: "…at Stebbing's…" We boarded the barge boat with two others, saying unseen 'hellos' in the 'privacy' of the night! Once out at the barge and on deck, we were 'Covid briefed' before being ushered below where a big pot of tea awaited. Not being a tea drinker, a mug of coffee was made especially for Christobel.

"Seating at the table is distanced…" one of the crew said, chuckling. I shall call her 'H' for this yarn. I grinned at her as I pulled two chairs closer together, quipping, "we woke up together, so…" and she laughed which broke the ice with the other two chaps who'd boarded with us. It was great to see they had a sense of humour! I sensed a good day. Talking to them, I soon learnt that they both sailed dinghies but had not sailed aboard a cruiser or anything like this great barge we were aboard. Like ourselves, both had contributed in various ways to the benefit of the trust's operation.

Once our refreshing beverage had been drunk, we were ushered on deck to prepare for departure. The new dawn was breaking away to the east. I was explaining something to Christobel when I heard a quiet voice say something. It was the skipper; he was looking in our direction. From the gloom I heard the request, "Can you pull the mainsheet and block out please…"

Waving a hand to acknowledge, I said, "Come along darling, that's us…" to Christobel, adding, "I'll grab the block…you feed the sheet…bring it with you too…" I smiled to myself noticing how she found the rope heavy. This was a different sort of sailing day!

Another call drifted our way as we hooked the block onto the main horse traveller, "Don't forget the mousing…" and I saw the skipper pointing. I looked quizzically, the spotted a length of line dangling from the mizzen forestay, by the wheel.

"Do you know what to do?" Christobel asked, looking at me. I nodded: although it was some years since I'd done it, probably aboard the *May Flower* during the family's last sail aboard her in 1974! A mousing is accomplished with a 'thin' bit of line and its tying was largely a common seamanship task. We pulled the sheet's slack in and made it off with a locking hitch.

We left the sheet tail in loops across the waist deck and then I wandered forward to give further help. I'd seen the skipper go aft and turning from completing a task saw that he was in deep discussion about something with Christobel. I was then busy helping drop off the mainsail's upper and lower brails, before becoming conscious of Christobel gesticulating to me. I wandered aft as she came forward towards me…

Christobel had a horrified look. "He wants me to take her away…" she burbled at me. "Said I wasn't sure…" she added, while looking aghast, a look even of pleading for help! Then she told of being 'quizzed' as to how she would leave the buoy too! I began to move away, smiling to myself. "Don't go…" I heard, said as if a command! "You do it…I'll watch…"

I could see the look on her face. She clearly wasn't going to do it. "Okay…" I said, grinning at her.

The skipper had gone forward for a 'conference' with his two crew, so I surveyed the river in Collier's Reach, gazed aloft to fix the wind direction and considered our position over on the eastern side where the trust had their mooring.

The skipper reappeared. Looking at the pair of us, he grinned. It felt almost as it was how he'd wanted it to be, but I wasn't sure…"Are we dropping off and then coming right round?" I asked decisively.

With a barely perceptible nod, I got my answer then he said, "Just let the foresail and topsail do the work…"

"Okay…"

"We'll sheet the main out as we come round…let her draw…just a bit of wheel…" I spun a couple of turns to starboard, catching the skipper's rising hand indicating enough. The barge began to forge ahead.

Dropping away from the buoy off Heybridge Basin.

I heard a quiet, "Glad you're doing this…" and I turned towards my mate and prodded her gently, grinning.

'Clear' a concise call floated from forward, telling us we were away.

"Just let her come…" and the mighty *Blue Mermaid* sweetly turned on her heel in a gracious sweep. As the barge came through the wind, the main brail was being let go. The skipper and Christobel heaved on the mainsheet, tighter than I'd expected. But of course, the 'corner' was coming up – Hilly Pool, a hard point on Northey Island. We knew this spot well from sailing on *Whimbrel* here many times. It was good thinking: it would have meant harder work within minutes.

The tide though seemed to be doing strange things. Its flow was threatening to take us into the moorings along Millbeach. There is a similar flow on the River Medway under Cockham Woods, on the ebb. It was fate accompli for, unless we made a change, of course, we'd go with the flow! I knew a tack was needed and mentioned it. Skipper and mate were looking at the eddies and the run of moored boats. There was a definite onshore set. A decision soon came. I was 'told' to tack. The skipper also called for the anchor to be made ready for a quick drop. As I heard the chain being piled on top of the windlass ready, I called, "Ready about…"

"Ready," I heard from forward, seeing a man on the foresail bowline ready…

"Lee O."

Looking aloft, I watched as the topsail softly slatted a couple of times until it had the air. "Le' go," I called loudly, as the skipper was telling me to bring the helm back smarter…I spun the wheel harder, before checking it. I was being given another quiet lesson.

Slowly, ever so slowly, the good ship gathered way, forging across the fairway, almost stemming the flow of the ebb, towards the Northey Island shore. Good ship she was, we made our ground and I was soon spinning the wheel a couple of turns only to bring the *Blue Mermaid* round again, to point downstream clear of Osea Island, towards a distant 'sliver of a gap' between the island and Stansgate Point on the south side of the river.

I was relaxing into the feel of this pedigree of the sea. She was doing everything I wanted her to do. Bloody marvellous! I don't ever remember being left alone at May Flower's wheel, but I had helmed aboard a number of barges over the last two decades – *Wyvenhoe* as mentioned, *Pudge, Centaur, Hydrogen* and the *Edith May* being others that come to mind. In the conditions, helming was no effort at all. (Later in a squall, when another was helming, it took an effort to hold her steady.) But for now, the ship seemed to relax too and as if to reinforce the feeling, a tray of tea was passed up from below.

After the minor moment of anxiety, I had noticed that 'H' the trust's fantastic stalwart, in all things that they do, had disappeared. She was 'number one mate', but the trust had a 'youngster', Ollie, who was more than capable. Ollie, I discovered, in conversation, is from the Northeast – not a noted spritsail barging area! I found him an absolute delight and he loved the life. I soon realised where 'H' had gone. Breakfast was underway: I caught the unmistakable and mouth-watering aroma of grilling bacon creeping up the aft cabin steps, close by me.

On a straight course downriver, we were making over the ebb nicely in a gathering morning air. "Right…" the skipper said, "we'll anchor just past the Doctor…" (This is a buoy off the southern side of Osea Island marking a fat belly of mud.) I knew the area and nodded in assent.

A little past the buoy, I tacked round. Hands were ready by the mainmast and the topsail head was let run and gathered in by our two friends. The foresail came down and was quickly moved clear of the windlass as the main brail winch was in operation gathering up the bulk of the huge, tanned mainsail. The skipper, with Christobel's help, was paying out the mainsheet in a controlled manner. Then, as we came head to wind, the anchor was let go. I watched the anchor man look over the side, walk back and let out more cable. We brought up nicely, snubbing to the ebb. After tidying, we were, in a timely fashion, called below for breakfast. I was glowing with exhilaration!

Cor, what a breakfast was placed before us. Lashings of it. Far too much – enough to feed a race crew! We weren't aboard to eat so, as soon as people had munched a sufficiency, we were being cajoled to move, but chatting is great too! There were a couple of digs! A little earlier, I'd noticed that Ollie had quietly disappeared. On deck we found him awaiting hands to help to lower the bowsprit and rig the jib, which he'd hauled up on deck and pulled from its bag.

A hearty breakfast below in the hold...

That done, we were deemed ready to go. Of course, it all takes longer but it would make a poor tale! During the rigging operation, we witnessed the big wooden barge, *Hydrogen*, owned by Topsail Charters sail past with all sail set. A lovely sight, not often seen. We saw her later up the Colne, as we passed the Bench Head in a stiffening breeze, cracking along at a pace.

Dawn had broken but looking back upriver towards Heybridge it was horribly grey and unappetising, however, away to the east, marching triumphant against the ebb was a largely blue sky, saying, surely, we were in for a splendid sun-filled day. And after the recent run of weather, it was the more pleasing. We were all busy for a while, hoisting and sheeting out the topsail and dropping off mains'l brails leaving it 'hanging' on the main...

"Set the mizzen please..." the skipper said to us both, puffing a little from taking up the mains'l sheet slack.

Earlier, the skipper had set it, but I had helped, doing an 'easy bit'. I quizzed with my eyes the 'tangle' of ropes at the base of the mast and sorted them all out. "Come on darling..." I said, handing

Christobel the sheet, remembering it was something she never had the chance to do aboard the *May Flower* all those years ago. "Just pull in the slack as it comes down…" I commented, reassuringly.

"Not too tight…" quietly floated our way from the skipper. The halyards and sheet were made off. Returning to an out of the way position clear of the wheel, another softly spoken comment was directed to me. "Okay, you take her away…"

Forward, the other two chaps were happily winding the windlass under the supervision of Ollie. Up and down, the foresail was hoisted and belayed with the windward bowline, to sail the barge round. We began to turn as the anchor was broken out…I could see the two chaps winding away laughing at the new ease they found! They were also being shown how to fleet the cable back across the windlass barrel for it has a natural tendency to walk to port as it is wound in.

Once round and on course down river, the jib was hoisted. *Hey, I thought, it's the first time I've sailed on a bowsprit rigged barge.* I sensed too that the eldest of my brothers would be dead jealous!

And as my previous thought began to recede, I remembered our father's 'bowsprit' which he'd intended fitting to the *May Flower* after he had renewed the barge's stem during 1959/60. The spar was used as a derrick to lift the heavy stem members, the inner apron and outer stem piece, into place during fitting. The barge had been a bowsprit rigged vessel for most of her trading life.

Never mind the past, here I was, a 'novice' being left to just get on with it and sail. The *Blue Mermaid* felt easy on the helm with her jib pulling nicely. It was 'simple' sailing, just a matter of the odd back and forth tweaking of the wheel, a bit like steering *Whimbrel* when she was in her groove. What an honour – even Christobel commented.

It was a joyous sail down river, past the moorings along the southern shore belonging to the river's 'middle clubs' and on to the moored red bulk of 'Radio Caroline' – a converted trawler. She didn't seem as big as when we sailed past in our 24-foot *Whimbrel*, but her tall slender aerials reaching skywards were the same.

Sitting beside me on the aft cabin top as I stroked the wheel, Christobel said, "You know, it's strange…"

Interrupting before she finished, I said, "What…" – a failing of mine!

"Well, it all looks different from up here…" and Christobel pointed at the Thirslet Spit Buoy, then towards the old ship and the distant shore. "Different from being on *Whimbrel*…" She was right. It was a vastly different perspective from being aboard our little clinker sloop. On this 'beast' our eyeline was at least two metres higher. Doesn't seem much, but noticeable.

The view aloft while I was facetime calling my mother.

I had booked a facetime call with my dear mother's care home, so as we came abreast of Bradwell's cocooned nuclear power station buildings I handed over to one of the other chaps, who gleefully took the wheel. It had been a subliminal period at the helm. As I talked to my mother, I showed her shots as I walked about the decks and up aloft at the sails – sights known well in former years aboard *May Flower*. It had been hard for my mother during the 2020 lockdown and she just seemed to 'wither and shrink' into herself – Covid Syndrome was the name given to the problem affecting many older people round the world. As time went on, a series of bad falls heralded the loss of her independence which had diminished greatly in any case. It was at this time, as a family, we decided that our mother would be best looked after by the caring profession. It was a sad decision, but for the best…

An hour later, we were thrashing along in a bit of a squall and I wandered about the deck taking pictures. The sky darkened considerably, quite quickly, although a lump of cloud had been watched for some time. I looked up at the lofty topmast seeing it flex and wondered how long the topsail would stay up.

As if to answer my thoughts, a short time later I heard a call, "Ready with the topsail." Then, almost immediately at a call, the head was dropped and clewed in tight. It remained sheeted out. Rucked, had long been the bargeman's term. The upper triangle from mast cap out to sprit end and topmast truck is removed, leaving a much smaller triangle giving the main sail plan a 'squared off' shape. It's an amazingly effective reef, just one of many quirks unique to the spritsail rig's versatility and ease of handling.

The squall produced a few spots of precipitation making me exceedingly glad of the decision to bring our foul weather gear and wearing it! It blew quite hard for a while after the cloud passed over and the bow was chucking up spray over the deck as we bashed through a growing bottom of Wallet chop. We sailed to as far as the Wallet Spitway Buoy with a bow wave foaming down along the barge's sides. Upon coming round on a long easy reach, the sky cleared away somewhat and tranquillity returned to the barge's motion and passage through the water.

The barge heeled gamely to the gusts…

In the distance, Sales Point and the ancient chapel of Saint Peter which sits close by on land running down into the saltings was a historic place of some significance. The chapel was built within the remains of a Roman Fort by monks from Lindisfarne who reintroduced Christianity to this part of Eastern England some fourteen hundred years ago.

Talking to one of our fellow crew, I pointed the chapel out for he had never been out in the open beyond the river proper or been to the chapel. Our intended anchorage for a late lunch lay on the northward face of the point. It was a delightful spot with good holding along a shingle and sand shore, often dotted with walkers. In the summer months, boats anchor off for picnics and dinghies with multi-coloured sails can be seen hauled up the beach. It is a wildlife spot, so care must be given…

Returning on deck after our lunch, the weather had returned to its earlier subliminal autumn self. The wind had dropped appreciably and the topsail was hoisted fully aloft. Our jobs were much as they were earlier and I felt honoured to take the *Blue Mermaid* away

Getting away after lunch.

again. My forward hands were our day's two companions, who stood the forewatch all the way upriver.

Clearing our anchorage off Sales Point, we reached deep into the River Blackwater, not needing to tack until off the old Tollesbury rail jetty remains, where a buoy had recently been positioned. I commented to Ollie about mud erosion causing the stumps becoming more prominent over recent years, enough to be considered a hazard. After another tack, the Thirslet Spit buoy sat 'in our way' forcing a tack. It was useful: after my next, I was able to fetch past Stone Point outside the yacht moorings and did not need another until up towards the Goldhanger Creek conical green. Ollie had lit and set the sailing lights by then. The light was fading. Dusk was rapidly coming up behind us, all sailors know the difference. The light ahead was still good enough.

It was about this time that I saw the barge's two crew in discussion with the skipper. Later, gaining an opportunity to ask 'H' what the problem was, she said, "Nothing…" adding, with a chuckle, "except you got us up here too quickly…"

Dusk came, side lamps were lit…

"Sorry…"

"Our normal guests wouldn't have…" she said, laughing. I think it was a compliment, but the nub of it was that we had to lose time for we were far too early on the flood to go on up to Heybridge. We were on a short tacking run down towards Lawling Creek and my two forehands continued with their sterling service on bowline duty. Clearing the Barnacle Buoy sitting off the creek, I eased the barge round to clear the Doctor, with the wind more abeam. I was told to sail up towards the Southey buoy and come about. We commenced to sail back and forth a few of times. The 'seaward' leg took longer against the flood, wasting 'my' time! It was while we sailed up and down, it got suddenly quite dark, black even…Eventually, with the barge's crew and our two shipmates keeping eyes on the blinking lights of the river's buoys, I was released to sail towards a distant light positioned ashore by the Blackwater Sailing Club. I had never done this aboard *Whimbrel*, never mind a ninety-foot barge of some 180 tonnes displacement!

I wasn't uneasy, but I felt somewhat pleased when the skipper appeared by my side. He didn't take over, but said, "Keep her going…" adding gently, "I'll take her as we come to Hilly Pool…"

"Understood," I said in response. There would be a series of short tacks between the Northey shore and the thick spread of moorings on the Heybridge bank. It was dark, but it was surprisingly easy to see 'what was what'.

The skipper took the helm, asking me to be ready to lift the port leeboard. I stood, handle in hand, ready. I knew the boards were blinking heavy! In the event, it took two of us to lift it…The skipper and Christobel did the starboard one as we tacked…she said afterwards, "Nearly did me in…had to work hard…" That, she did!

The working of the barge and the honed training of the crew made it seem so easy as the skipper eased the *Blue Mermaid* round on the first 'Heybridge' tack.

"Stow the mizzen please…" the skipper quietly asked. We did it as quickly as we could.

After several rapid short tacks, the topsail came down. The foresail followed as the barge came round, to jog back towards her mooring buoy. This was all played out as if in slow motion, controlled, man in tune with machine.

I was sent forward to haul on the mains'l lowers with 'H' while another wound the main brail winch. Christobel was easing the main sheet…and all the time the skipper was watching the speed of the mighty *Blue Mermaid* as she slowly forged virtually sail-less over the flood.

Forward, the waiting mate, Ollie, was calling back instructions to the skipper. Then, flexing with a positive lean outboard, the long boathook lance-like in his strong arms, he deftly picked up the long trailing line flowing in the tide from its eye on the mooring buoy. "Got it…" he called succinctly. Shortly afterwards there was an almost imperceptible 'snub' as the barge brought up, moored, then slowly, she fell back with the flow of the flood, signalling the end of a grand day's sailing!

In the quiet of the gathering night, we alighted from the barge's boat and walked towards where we'd left our car. Our friends followed, chattering, as we were. All agreed what a wonderful day we'd had.

The two chaps, members of a 'group' were planning a further sail the following year. Good on them. We said our goodbyes…they'd been great shipmates. Thanks fellas!

Next day, awaking with aches in places I felt I shouldn't, I was still glowing inwardly. Outwardly too, I was told! Christobel was brimming with enjoyment too but also remarked on some 'funny' aches!

Thank you, Sea-Change Sailing Trust, for such a memorable day. "What a team…"

11
Short but Sweet, with Two 'Grahams'...

My eldest sibling was over from his home in Canada visiting family and generally having a good time – something he is good at! He'd cleverly 'booked' a sail during the planning stage of the trip, tying all together. It was still early in the season, I suppose, but we had at least moved into the first week of June.

Before my brother's arrival, a plot was hatched with a friend who had been coming away sailing for a number of years, during a convivial dinner evening. The chap had often enjoyed at least one trip a year, sometimes two. "I'll come..." he said, at my proposal for a four-day cruise. A nod of 'approval' came from his lovely wife sitting between us!

"It would be weather permitting," I explained, "we can take an outside trip round the east end of the Isle of Sheppey to Harty Ferry."

"Nice pub too..." my friend said, grinning.

"Then we'll hit Queenborough, Upnor then home," I finished saying about the plan in mind.

So, in a seemingly short time forwards, my brother arrived to stay with us a few days before the planned sailing event. He got the 'visit treatment' – Maldon, West Mersea and Tollesbury, I think too.

Sailing day arrived. The early morning forecast had a bit of a puff in it, but overall, it was due to settle into a north north-easterly giving a decent sailing breeze. My brother, Graham, was detailed to deal with rowing the dinghy down the creek to *Whimbrel*, while my friend, another Graham (I'll suffix him with a D when needed) and I took the stores and bags to the boat. Some will have cottoned onto a looming hitch – trouble for the skipper too, perhaps...

We got away by mid-morning and were on a beam reach as soon as the sails were set. There was 'something' though, I detected when asking for something to be done, but couldn't cotton onto what. The same thought came to me later too. The only excitement of the passage happened very early on when the pleasure 'steamer' *Balmoral* passed across our bow, sufficiently clear, but close enough for me to 'order' a course change. It was unprofessional, I thought. She was a grand sight indeed, her deck's packed with passengers in bright summery colours.

As time moved on, I prepared our lunch, whilst the crew got on with sailing the boat. I seem to remember dropping a couple of pork pies in the shopping trolley for our first lunch. Graham D always arrived with a stack of stuff, arranged by his good wife. Passing out a bowl of cut pie and another of tomatoes and cucumber wedges, I said, "Mustard…" passing it into a hand that appeared in my line of sight.

The crew…

We munched as the coast of Sheppey peeled away to our starboard side. I smiled, contentedly, for it was clear the pairing was working a treat. I was soon to find out quite how well too, but not in the way I expected. "We'll clear up later…" I said, "when we've had some tea."

Progress was grand and by a little after two in the afternoon, we were gybing inside the Columbine Buoy, freeing the sheets onto a broad reach. It was clear that we were continuing to make good time over the ebb too.

A little after four in the afternoon we swished past the Receptive Buoy on the lower edge of the Horse Sand, I said, "Okay, we'll sail onto a buoy I know I can use…on the south side." Both chaps nodded. "Graham, I'll rig the buoy line…" I was directing the comment to my brother, but they both looked at me, smiling.

That done, I dropped the halyards onto the deck and placed the mainsail ties ready to hand. I can't remember who was helming, but they had been pretty good at 'sharing' during the trip, with odd periods allowed to me! This is something I don't mind. It was and remains one of my joys to give my crews a free hand.

Over the top of the uncovered sands, a spritsail barge could be seen enjoying a bit of a 'romp', well ahead of us. I thought the cut of her rig shouted out, "*Mirosa*…" and, sure enough, it was, we saw later. On top of the sands, the two boys enjoyed looking at the large colony of seals that have 'rested' in that spot for more years than I can remember.

The wind had eased after we sailed past the Receptive – we were shielded by the bulk of the Harty Island's 'lump' from the breeze. Judging it time for a hand to be forward, I said, "Graham, you do the buoy…" I wanted the other to helm. Thinking he was still on the helm, I gazed round the anchorage for a few seconds, spotting a friend's boat moored not far from where we were bound.

I suddenly realised, as *Whimbrel* luffed up, that both boys had gone forward, one to port and the other to starboard! Grabbing the vacant tiller and chuckling, I realised 'the something' – two 'Grahams' aboard clearly meant trouble! I left them to it…The mate, 'stuck' at home, would have a good laugh too, later, when I called her, I was sure of that.

They moored without a hitch, but I had a horrible suspicion that plots were afoot…'Tea?' I heard one of the crew ask, just as I was putting the last lashing on the mainsail and tying back the halyards.

"Yes please," I said, calling below where the pair had disappeared.

"Cake too?" the other queried.

"Please…"

We were all sorted and settled round the little cockpit table I made many years before, when my mobile rang. It was a sailing friend on his catamaran inviting us all over for a beer. It was agreed for around six as we were planning to go ashore to the Ferry Inn. That didn't leave much time. Even if the crew didn't want one, I needed a face wash – salt and sunscreen is an obnoxious combination when it gets into the eyes!

After stopping off and enjoying a beer with the chap who had called me, we rowed ashore, well I did, strangely. Leaving the dinghy on a long line to her anchor we walked up the rickety hard, past the old ferry winch and up the hill to the Inn. "No, we haven't booked," one of the Grahams said.

"You happy outside?" was the next question. I quickly nodded.

Retreating to an outside table, basked in evening sunshine, with our pints of ale and the menu, we supped and chatted. A waitress came out and took our order, which was nice.

"The tide will be rising while we're here," I said, adding, "the dinghy will need to be looked at…" looking at my crew!

"I'll go…" one said.

"I'll come too…" the other chirped, in accord. They both went. Not quite hand in hand! I took the opportunity to call 'the mate' for she was always the mate whoever was aboard *Whimbrel*…during our chat, I said, "I've got a couple of clowns aboard…"

"Valerie and I have already discussed this…" Christobel responded, laughing. Right. Women, eh!

The two boys were ages…getting back well after their starters had arrived! It was an excellent meal, enjoyed with a couple of ales. The evening was setting in and an after-glow of the day's largely missing sun had put striking colour over the Kent hills. Alas, it was soon time we headed back down the hard to where the dinghy was found riding to her anchor much further up than where we'd landed. I got my brother to row back. It was probably his longest row for two years. Bless him.

All aboard the ship awoke late. It was past nine. Breakfast was hastily got under the grill for a crew with empty bellies is an unhappy one. Graham cooked and the other cleared up!

We were bound for Queenborough and just before ten, we dropped the mooring and began tacking, westward, towards Elmely Ferry. The wind was from the north-westerly direction, so we enjoyed long and shortboards, using up much of the tide-filled Swale's width. The Swale is a grand place to sail in, especially towards high water when channel buoys can be largely 'ignored' somewhat. With the tide lifting us nicely too, we made short work of the distance.

The day started a bit grey and overcast but brightened as the morning fell into the afternoon. It wasn't a sparkling late spring day, for sure, but was pleasant enough for sailing.

Coming up towards the Sheppey Bridge and listening to the calling channel, I heard a ship talking to the bridge keeper. She was leaving Ridham Dock at that moment. "Put the engine on…" I said to neither one nor the other. It was started.

We motor sailed onwards as I called the bridge to alert them of our need to pass through too. "Follow on behind…" was the order, so within 15 minutes after starting the engine, we were through. I silenced the mechanical noise!

Reaching Queenborough Harbour, I called the duty harbour operative and was assigned a 'decent' buoy. "We'll sail on past and drop the main," I said to my crew. Off the pylons marking the burnt remains of the town's old ferry pier, the crew brought *Whimbrel* round through the wind while I dropped and stowed the mainsail. We then ran back to the mooring, where it was deftly picked up by one of the capable crew.

A call to the liberty (ferry) boat and we were soon heading ashore for some supper. Over a beer, I said, "We'll leave about ten in the morning and take a trip upriver through the inner passages…" adding, to fill in some detail, "Stangate, Milfordhope Creek, through by Shoregate, under Nore Marsh Island and Hoo passages…" Upnor was our planned mooring for the night, at the invitingly friendly Medway Yacht Club.

It was a delightful morning and we sailed off in a northerly air to tack out of the West Swale into the River Medway. The crew got everything ready, together, then they let go of the buoy on my signal.

They did everything together…

Out in the river, I saw one of the funniest things ever seen aboard *Whimbrel*. My brother, I noticed, had begun to 'hog' the tiller. I said something and glancing aft from where I was a few moments later, I saw Graham D endeavouring to peel Graham's fingers away from the firm grip he had on the tiller…I just burst into laughter, quickly snapping the scene with my camera, catching the moment with *Twitch* obediently following in our wake!

We ran down the length of Stangate, bathed in sunshine and turned west into the creek's basin-like bottom. The helm was asked to take the northerly 'gap' into Milfordhope Creek. "Timing is about right…" I said, "plenty of water to go straight through." I was referring to the 'Shoregate Gap' of course. The gap was much narrower and shallower when my brother and I were youngsters growing up in this neck of the woods. Graham had seen the area a few times since 'disappearing' off to Canada to marry his sweetheart, but hadn't, as far as he could remember, been through for probably close to four decades.

"Crikey!" Graham exclaimed. "What's all that grass?"

"Ah, the area has silted over the years and cord grass took hold…" I explained, "trouble is the grass helps hold even more silt…"

He spotted the narrow channel threading up through the grass into Shoregate Dock, saying, "Blimey…"

"Over to starboard a bit…" I said, as the helm too began to look elsewhere rather than the narrow weed-infested gut we were heading through. He looked overboard at some bladderwrack waving nonchalant-like within touching distance and grinned.

Crossing the entrance to Otterham Creek, I said, "Lunch…"

Without further comment, both 'Grahams' dropped below and began preparing our sustenance. Both heads popped up, swivelling together in the small hatch space, for a spot of noisy excitement as a group of mini hovercraft skimmed away to one side of us, drivers bent on enjoying themselves enclosed in tight cockpits, helmeted heads and ear mufflers! I was enjoying a session at the helm of my boat, watching the world pass by, revelling in the colours of land, marsh and water changing in the passing of odd clouds over a predominantly blue sun-filled sky. But I watched below too, from time to time. I saw thick-cut slices of ham were deftly wedged into rolls with lashings of mustard on those who wanted it. Soon, individual plates were being handed to me, decorated with quartered tomatoes and thick-sliced cooling cucumber. "What a team," I murmured silently.

We ate as we slipped along on the underside of Nore Marsh Island. I pointed out where the farm cottage probably sat and the remnants of a timber wharf. A stray way, hard, once ran across to the island from the Gillingham shore. Sheep were the farm's mainstay. The tides were nearing springs and the saltings were flooded. After a being bathed in saltwater, a heady saline air hangs above the growth. "Smell that…" I said, breathing in deeply.

"Straight on across the Medway," I said, pointing to the distant moorings where several spritsail barges were moored. I love this passage. It's full of interest. It is well buoyed and is fun. It weaves through Hoo Middle Creek, which leads into the barge moorings, a yard and the Hundred of Hoo Sailing Club, but we were eschewing all of that and continuing west into West Hoo Creek and out over the Hoo mud flats.

I pointed out the near tide covered remains of the west country fruit schooner, the *Rhoda Mary*, which my brother and I had played on as kids in the late 1950s and early1960s. At the time we passed her, there were all sorts of discussions going on by a group 'down west' who wanted to raise the remains and 'rebuild' her. It was a pipe dream, I thought, for it would make more sense to build a replica out of steel. Ah well...

We threaded out into the main run of the river as soon as we could, or we would have been trapped inside the moorings for some distance and be at the 'mercy' of tide borne forces rather than the breeze under the heavily wooded slopes that reach down to the water along here.

The crew knew where we were going and one of them was doing a stint. I only had to mention keeping away from the mooring trot a couple of times and 'watch the tide flow...' for a lack of concentration can find you setting down onto an obstruction all too quickly. We were sailing up to Rochester Bridge, just for the hell of it!

"Look," I said, as we rounded St Mary's Point opposite Upnor, "the *Edith May*..." and there she was, coming off the pontoon by the lock, loaded with afternoon tea 'sailors' on a trip downriver. I watched as the topsail was sheeted to the sprit-head and then the sail's headstick rise carrying the sail gracefully aloft against an azure sky.

We eventually ran towards Rochester's cluster of low-level bridges, tacking round close up to retrace our inward passage. I had to take the helm for neither Graham was concentrating sufficiently, allowing the tide to 'grab' the boat, causing a missed heart beat! It was an enjoyable tack back down Chatham Reach to Upnor, where we moored to a vacant buoy.

While we were having tea, the *Edith May* sailed past, luffing up towards the moorings off St Mary's Point to allow a ship to pass, starboard to starboard which must have been agreed between them! Soon after, my brother was off in *Twitch* for an hour's sail. Just before he pushed off, I said, "Don't forget the tide's run here..."

"Yes skip..." he said, pulling a face, as if to say, I've not forgotten. The other Graham laughed, then we settled back, chatted and watched the world go on round us. A huge number of dinghies began returning from their down-river races. At times the classes seemed to be all mixed up. They were followed by a fleet of Hunter Sonata's, a superb little racer. Graham D was amazed at the number of crew on them, ranging from three, four and up to five.

At an appointed moment, we all readied ourselves for a run ashore. "A couple of good pubs…" I said, with much enthusiasm. Graham D nodded in assent.

My brother chipped in with "I know…" while licking his lips.

We stopped at the club for a pint as a thank you for the use of a mooring before moving on. The Ship Inn provided another tasty beer. They weren't doing food though. "Heck!" I exclaimed, saying, "Two more pubs in Upper Upnor…" So we supped up and walked rather rapidly in their direction.

Arriving hot and rather short of breath we found, one after the other, that food for the day was finished. I had a trump card. "There's the other one on the waterfront…" but I'd not been inside the place for years! Reaching the last chance saloon, we found it too had just ceased food serving!

"Right…" I said, jovially, "plenty of food aboard the boat…pasta, sauces, various tinned fish, luncheon meat etc…" knowing that hungry bellies wouldn't be a hindrance. Rowing back to *Whimbrel*, I realised that I should have asked to speak to the chef at the last pub: they'd have sold me some stuff, surely!

We were all in good spirits back aboard. There was much mirth over 'being caught out' – I'd not even got an onion aboard! I gave the crew glasses and a fresh wine box, then got on with digging out what was in the locker.

I was suddenly aware of a bit of a kerfuffle out in the cockpit. The second funniest thing seen on the trip confronted me. Two grown men were clearly struggling with getting anywhere with opening the wine box. I burst out laughing. The pair turned and looked, faces like little boys as if to say 'What?'

I relieved them of the job and said, "Pour me one please…" It took three separate hands to do that job. I shook my head in wonderment…A glass was eventually handed over and I took a sip, well, a lug, a long pull actually and then I got on with our supper preparations. Fish was vetoed!

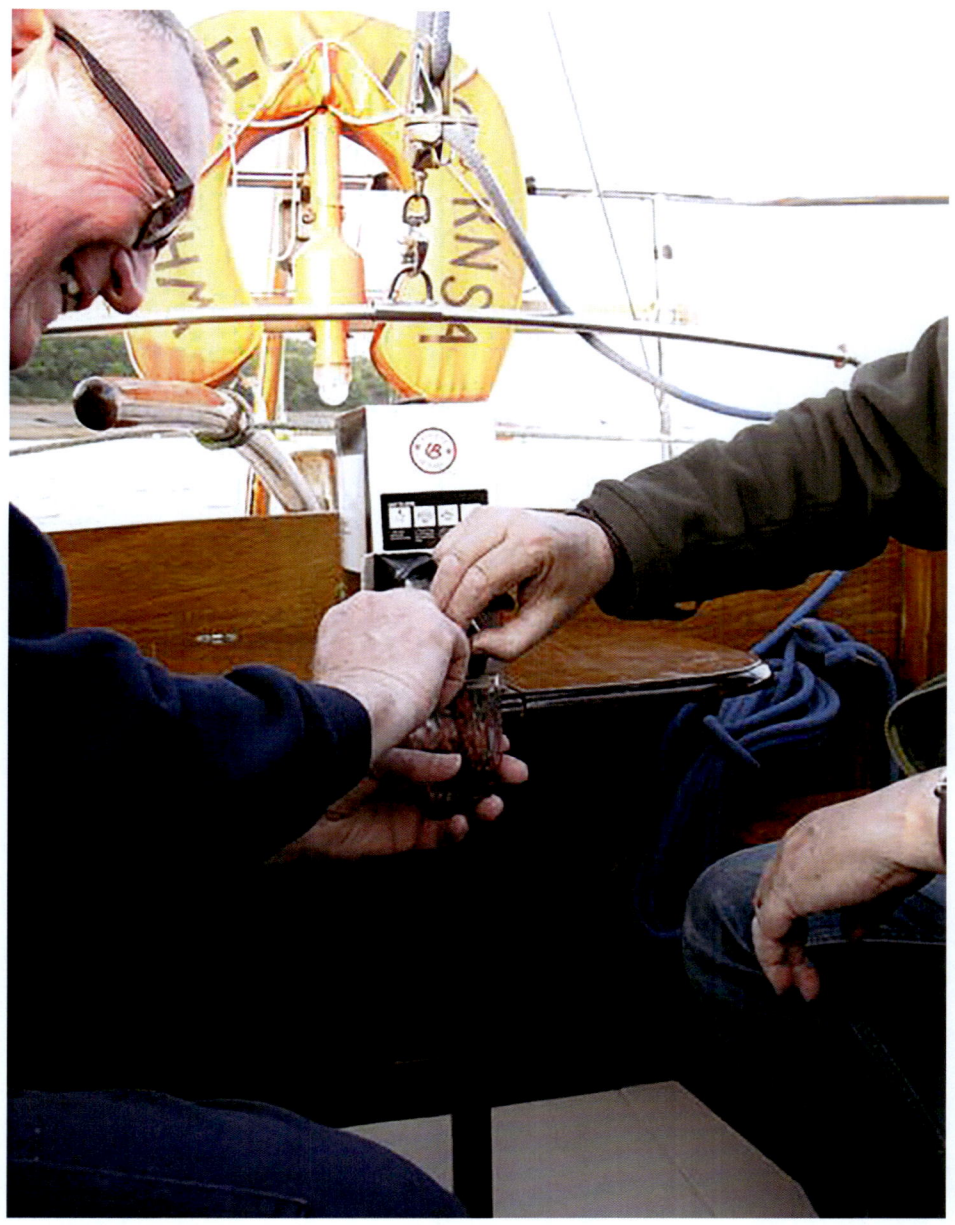

Two make 'light' work...

Every now and then two heads grinned down at me from the cockpit. They were ignored. In time, I neared the point of being ready to serve. It being a gorgeous evening, I passed cutlery, condiments and a big bowl of grated cheese out to helpful hands.

Ah yes, at the end of the meal, both of my crew stated they'd enjoyed the finest meal for a long time. I wrote it up in the logbook and both initialled the comment. I'd got my own back on them!

The next day we set off under mainsail and engine until breakfast of bacon rolls was cooked and cleared away. Then we settled into a scintillating sail down the River Medway in a stiff, at times, north-easterly. The direction meant a dead beat up some of the reaches, but we made the entrance a little after low water, feeling exhilarated.

A couple of hours later we fetched up off my creek's entrance, dropped sails and picked up the club waiting buoy. Sails stowed and boat tidied, it wasn't long before there was sufficient tide to creep in and berth.

Looking about me as we motored in, I was feeling elated with what was the last sail of spring, "Summer's here," I stated emphatically: I saw only a couple of brent geese along the salting edge. The overwintering bulk had at last flown…

12
Whimbrel with a Kiwi Aboard...

"I've never seen Iken Church from the water..." Paul wrote in an email, long before he arrived from 'down-under' for an English summer away from a Kiwi winter.

Paul has sailed aboard *Whimbrel* on several occasions when over from his long-time home in far off New Zealand's north island. Essex born, he reappears from time to time, usually with a full programme arranged through his many contacts, round England's eastern waterways.

During his previous visit, he had achieved a long-held wish to get up close to an old 'Thames racer' the famous *Veronica*. I watched, smiling, as he'd physically 'caressed' her weather-worn stem. It was about all that remains of her once proud bow where she rests in her marshland grave. He was also able to wave a fond 'farewell' to the distant smudge of the equally famous *Sirdar* languishing in her own cord grass grave, not so far away. Our trip had been a little marred by some inclement weather for mid-summer, but Paul is from hardy stock.

We had sailed the Medway's 'inner' passages. We popped into Lower Halstow for a pint and a sandwich, sailed through 'the gap' past the old farm dock at Shoregate and round the inner side of Nor Marsh Island then through the Middle and West Hoo creeks. We'd finished with a spin down to Rochester Bridge before sailing back downriver to find a mooring at Medway Yacht Club.

The next day we'd pottered down to Queenborough, nattering about the river's changes over the years Paul had been 'away'. After mooring, we'd had a walk for stores, enjoying fish and chips ashore. A prompt return to our little ship was needed for we'd an early start.

The following day, we had an enjoyable 'romp' across the estuary, down the Swin and across the spit way bound for the Colne. We anchored in Pyefleet for the night. Our shopping expedition of the previous day meant we dined sumptuously on thick-cut Barnsley Chops, marinaded in wine, garlic and rosemary – my crew remembers that meal to this day!

Our little cruise had ended in Bradwell after a night in 'The Quarters' off West Mersea, where Paul enjoyed a pint of beer sitting on a bench chair dedicated to the life of one of his favourite reads, the author, Maurice Griffiths!

However, back to where we were. In a general way, I earmarked a slot with favourable tides to enter the Ore and Alde, which, of course must be considered. A thumbs up and 'noted in diary' came winging back, so it was booked into *Whimbrel's* family summer sailing calendar.

Paul was fully aware that I'd encountered a health problem having been diagnosed with prostate cancer that year and an awful lot depended on outcomes, well beyond my control. Undaunted, I remained completely optimistic throughout the first half of that year, believe me, it was the only pathway!

My crew in his 'happy place'...

I had no qualms at all: Paul has had many years of sailing experience and I have found him to be a sound shipmate. Back home, he down-sized some years ago to a Farr design trailer-sailer, in which he mostly sails alone. He's part of an active 'live-wire' like-minded group sailing protected coastal waters and on the many inland lakes within New Zealand's North Island interior.

This trip of ours would be far more adventurous than his previous long cruise he'd enjoyed aboard *Whimbrel* and would, of course, be very weather dependent. With plans to enter and leave the River Alde up the Suffolk coast on consecutive days, this would be especially so. He understood all of this when we planned it all – me in a typical English winter and he in a semi-tropical summer.

The mate and I arrived in Bradwell the day before my new crew was due aboard, to enable our laundry to be cleared. It was towards the end of what had been a good August and the forecast was benign. The following day was glorious as if to reiterate the point. Paul arrived with his lovely wife Shona, who would drive their hire car back to their base. After a welcome, stowing of kit and stores brought along, we enjoyed coffee and a chat.

I began to clock watch and the girls departed. Later, I heard that Christobel took Shona on a tour via Bradwell's air force memorial upon which a number of New Zealanders are named.

So, soon after a boat briefing, our lines were slipped just before noon. Creeping through the moorings in Bradwell Creek sail was set and we then enjoyed an uneventful passage to Brightlingsea. On the way, the stately spritsail barge *Centaur* passed us, inbound for Maldon. As always, Paul was free to do as he wished and he was soon making a tweak here and another there – always the keen Kiwi sailor, I've grown to admire.

That Kiwi keenness was tested soon after our arrival at Brightlingsea. Upon mooring, I said, "the tender's bottom needs scrubbing."

"Right…" Paul said, looking at me digging out brush and bucket.

"Come on…" I said, hopping onto the pontoon, "once *Twitch's* bottom has been cleaned, we'll have some tea…"

Wielding the bucket and the meaningful scrubbing brush, my crew made short work of it, while I held the little boat rolled onto its sides, in turn. Sadly though, the meaningful scrubbing brush got swished 'overboard', when rinsing the bucket.

Over a pot of tea, we watched a coastal freighter berthing at the harbours wharf and the spritsail barge *Dawn* puttering under power. Brightlingsea is a busy little harbour with fishing boats, offshore wind farm tenders and occasional freighters coming and going, never mind a myriad of yachts and dinghy fleets scudding about.

I had a rest and later, over a beer, we toasted 'Iken or bust…' the pet name given to this cruise some many months before.

Scrubbing the dinghy's bottom!

Rowing back in the tender after our supper ashore, we both gazed upon a wondrous sunset. Gliding along, towards the bottom of the tide, all about us was enchantment. We were serenaded by the haunting cries of curlews and a myriad of waders feeding along the tide edges. Our planned departure was early, so after ensuring our readiness, the bunks were soon listening to the soft and gentle wheeze of our slumbering's…

The alarm screamed, louder than the piecing call of an

oystercatcher. I was jerked awake. Pulling on my shorts, I put the kettle on. Sliding back the main hatch and looking outside I saw that it was windless, but the sky was aglow with a fresh day. Awaiting the kettle's call, I reduced our moorings to two and streamed the tender astern. The kettle sang. "Tea…" I called.

Paul's arm appeared from forward, grabbing his mug. "I'm awake…" and rubbing his eyes, he grinned broadly.

Out on deck, we had a brief discussion and were quickly away, clearing Brightlingsea beacon an hour before high water. Looking astern, eastwards, as I hoisted the mainsail, a fiery orange ball had lifted above the horizon in a glorious fashion. I caught the glowing ball on the end of the *Dawn's* cocky sprit with my camera.

With the tide on the turn, we sneaked round Colne Point and we were in the grip of ebbing flow, helping us on our way. Paul had cast a look towards me, the evening before when I talked through my passage plan. "It's my usual route with enough tide," I said, grinning and had added, "Why go miles to the south before making the turn into the Wallet…loads of depth?" tapping the chart.

Once in the Wallet, a faint breeze assisted the throb of the diesel. "Breakfast…" I said, patting my midriff. My crew gave a thumbs up and the bacon was soon sizzling beneath the grill. We were soon munching bacon rolls as the boat with a comfortable gyrating motion made passage northwards over a low swell.

Our only 'moment' came when a large yacht 'chased up our stern' and swept closely down one side. He was on autopilot, not keeping a proper lookout. Perhaps he wanted to have a look at us, but that would have been kind: her skipper seemed oblivious. My crew, in what I discovered was a typical response, uttered something in Kiwi slang, which would best be left untranslated!

On the way, I said that I couldn't remember using the engine for such a long period, but we had a tidal gateway to meet, so needs must. When I later recounted our trip to my mate, her eyebrows lifted in mock surprise: it was five whole hours. Some miles before reaching Orford Haven, we were sailing along serenely with a silenced engine.

"Now," I said, as we both quizzed the pilotage chartlet, "reality bares no relation to our chart, so…" Chart and certainly the satnav unit were ignored as we located visually the buoys we were to follow. Seeing a yacht leaving she boosted any trepidations felt. Bars can be different from one day to the next. So, we swept past the Weir Buoy with an hour of the flood. Paul was grinning with sheer delight.

The bar was quiet, not surprising in the calm conditions, but a heave along the shingle was a reminder of what lay waiting if a mistake were made with any wind adding to one's woes. In glorious sunshine we sailed in, carried to a large extent by the sweep of the flood. It was a delight. There was some movement on the river of varying craft and a lovely little barge-yacht sailed down towards us with a large family group aboard, but, for a weekend, it seemed too quiet for such a day in holiday time.

The Butley River was our planned anchorage for the night and we enjoyed a pleasant sail to finish the passage nicely. We rounded up under the main and the anchor splashed overboard. Within moments, almost, after anchoring off Boynton Dock, Paul was away in *Twitch*, *Whimbrel's* lug-rigged tender. Upon his return, I was able to get a go too!

Later, over afternoon tea, Paul commented on the noticeable lack of birds. This was a phenomenon my mate and I had witnessed on previous visits: in comparison with our more local waters round the Lower Thames, Medway and Swale, it was starkly observable. Perhaps it was the time of year. Clearly, my crew was surprised for he'd been told to 'watch out for the birds…' There were a few gulls floating about and the odd oystercatcher. We did see numerous sleek seals swimming in the water and basking on the mud banks during our separate ganders in the tender.

That evening we enjoyed a brace of lamb chops that Paul had brought aboard, frozen, marinated in red wine, rosemary and garlic, a *Whimbrel* special and Paul's favourite. It was washed down with a glass or two, as we again toasted 'Iken or Bust'. We were all but there!

The next day dawned in glorious fashion with a mysterious mistiness over the marshland sitting low behind the grass-covered wall. It was caused, surely, by the warm morning sun drawing the land's moisture out. We sailed off our anchorage and worked up past Orford, where the town's ancient castle, dominated the riverscape and land in the manner its builders wanted. Fortunately, the swain's sword and his violence had long departed so our lives were safe and we sailed freely by!

Closing Aldeburgh, we lost the wind and the engine was started for it was nearing highwater. Passing through the moorings, another sister Finesse, the *Sandpiper*, was seen. I had earlier pointed out a rare and now the only Finesse 27, *Tugela*, moored down off Orford Quay. It's always grand to see one of *Whimbrel's* sisters…later, while navigating carefully along the torturous withy-marked channel we passed another, *Catharine 1*, a twenty-one-foot version and cameras clicked at each other across the calm sunlit water. Today, we had been charmed.

Once clear of the Aldeburgh moorings, the panorama becomes a vista of wide, open, water, but as I said to Paul, "Now we must follow the withies, or…"

"Don't want to do that…" he said, laughing, knowing I was thinking of glutinous mud.

As we passed by some private moorings, I pointed out the old brickworks wharf which sits at 'the back' of Aldeburgh. Away to port was Cob Island. In actuality, the island is no longer really one – just a sand-fringed patch of salt marsh. It has always been, to my mind, the likely candidate that featured as a picnic beach in Libby Purves's wonderful summer tale, *Regatta*. I've never asked any local people what their thoughts were about this!

Reaching Troublesome Reach, my crew was beginning to hop up and down like a little boy. Closing the area under Iken's St Botolph's Church, he went forward with his camera to gaze and drink in the wondrous view.

Approaching Iken church.

I love both of these rivers, but the lower reaches, except off Orford and the little Butley River, are in many respects similar to 'The Burnham River', in that little can be seen beyond the sea walls when the tide is low. It is only in the upper reaches an appreciation of the shallow valley's beauty can be properly savoured.

"We'll have to turn," I called softly to my crew, "tide turned nearly an hour ago…" In truth, I was twitching more than a little and memories of a being mud-bound a few seasons earlier seemed very fresh! So, we turned back towards Aldeburgh where a visitor's mooring was found and we high-tailed ashore for a walk into town, a light lunch at the yacht club and a shower was enjoyed too.

Later, we sailed slowly down to Orford, nattering, eventually mooring to a buoy with an orange pick-up as advised on my new Imray chart's harbour notes. Big Mistake! The harbour master promptly ranged alongside and chastised us, in no uncertain terms. We were banished to the 'detention buoys' it seemed far away back upriver to the northern end. Ashore, the Jolly Sailor was far more accommodating with a fine fish supper and a warm welcome.

Sometime later, I mentioned this kafuffle to a sailing friend and bingo, they'd had a similar experience. I found it strange: I'd not had a problem at Orford before.

After a leisurely breakfast 'Kiwi-style' cooked by my crew, we crept down Narrow Cuts on an idyllic morning. We were Pin Mill bound. I dug out the cruising chute and it gave us greater speed, well, I thought so! It was so quiet, I streamed astern in dinghy on a long line to capture *Whimbrel's* ultimate weapon at work. Paul thought it amusing to send an electronic message to all and sundry on his social media page depicting 'the skipper banished to the naughty corner...' Very funny, indeed!

Quietly out of the Orford River.

We enjoyed an uneventful passage to Languard Point, then through Harwich Harbour and up the Orwell. I pointed to the hills, chuckling: I find these soft rounded hills very reminiscent of the curves found on the Three Graces statue. We were soon in amongst the rows and rows of moorings. 'Where to…?' Paul asked as we came in under the steeply wooded backdrop on our final approach to Pin Mill.

"As close to the hard as possible," I said, looking intently through the moorings with my binoculars. I spotted a gap. "Near that bawley…" I smiled, for I knew she was moored close by the hard. "We'll sail on," I added, grinning at Paul. Classically, we fetched onto a buoy. As the sails slatted and fell to the deck, *Whimbrel* swung to point into the tide's flow surrounded by many wooden sisters.

The ship was soon tidied from our passage mishmash, for tea had been enjoyed downriver and we settled to a welcome glass of bottled ale. "Cheers…" Paul said, beaming brightly for he had caught the sun. It was a fine precursor to our supper ashore at the Butt and Oyster.

The tide was 'right' for the floating pontoon, saving us a 'slosh' up the tide-washed and oft muddy hard. And too saving someone the job of looking after the tender as the tide rose further. In my book, it is the crew's responsibility, except when with my mate: it being mine!

The 'Butt' has remained one of the pleasantest of waterside taverns there could possibly be, even allowing for its popularity with people from further afield for in past times it was essentially been a waterfront-mongers haunt. We had a good wholesome supper with a view out across the river, plus, of course a couple of the local brews. Leaving, the welcoming lights of the Pin Mill Sailing Club were spotted. My crew desired to visit, he said jovially, "I've come a long way for this." Far be it for me to prevent such an activity, I thought, as I savoured a further glass of ale. There was a bit of a 'sailors sing-song'. My crew dived, heartedly in, whilst I listened…but thinking of the next morning's planned early departure, I soon drank up and attracted my crew's attention, "we should go…"

Soon after sunrise, we dropped away from our friendly buoy under the engine with our mainsail set. There were a few zephyrs under the trees but not enough to properly get going. Time was against us. Another scorching day was clearly already settling in. The 'famous' (engineless) spritsail barge *Cambria* came off her berth under tow and it was a delight to watch her setting sail as she passed by under the ancient, wooded hillside. A timeless sight, indeed, as we slowly followed in her wake, both tacking seawards with the barge always just ahead.

In Harwich Harbour, I said, "It's no good…we'll have to motor…" My crew nodded for he too was conscious of the time. We could have had a glorious drift and a change of destination at any other time, but we had to get on southwards. We crept on and as expected, outside Harwich Harbour, there was barely a breath and what there was seemed hard on the bow, so the engine was started again.

It was clearly one of those weeks, so, I said, "Brightlingsea…" adding, "no point in going further west in this." My crew could only concur and he dutifully doused the headsail as the diesel rumbled into life. West Mersea had been our plan!

Motoring past The Naze, it was so quiet the water body clearly felt this too for the bottom was visible. Paul checked the depth. "Four metres," he said with some surprise. A crab pot came into view then a whole line of pots strung out, the line snaking between them. "Unmarked float to starboard…" Paul called, keeping a good lookout. There was a profusion of unmarked floats bobbing about in the heave of the sea. The tide was into its flood by then.

We cruised leisurely, close inshore, past Walton, Frinton, the low seawall hiding Holland Haven and onto Clacton. We discussed the coast's changes, the way spritsail barges brought most of what was needed to build these places over a century ago. "Holland Haven," I said, pointing across the water to a long dark line of a concrete faced wall. "Millions have been spent over there…"

"When?"

"A few years ago, now…to think there was once a haven for shipping!"

Up on the hill above what would have been the 'havens' northern shore, the old village church looked down on us. Close by, I knew, sat The Ship Inn. There has remained a line of such named ale houses, inland from the shore.

I was below preparing lunch when I caught a camera shot of Paul, helming. It's a classic 'happiness' picture of a man without a care in the world doing something he loved…

Later, by then early afternoon, Paul was below making tea. At the helm, I felt a ruffle on my cheek, as if it had been caressed. Then, the water's surface round us lost its oily smoothness and rippled like when testing setting jam. "Breeze…" I shouted. Paul shot from below and dived forward to hoist our Genoa. We were sailing with some conviction almost immediately. And with that breeze we closed Colne Point, nipping round the corner again and sailed serenely up to Mersea Stone where our sails were stowed.

The 'enforced' second visit to Brightlingsea gave Paul the chance to enjoy a farewell drink with an old Leigh-on-Sea pal who lived close to the harbour. A pleasant, friendly chap who knew of me, back to my childhood days, of my parents too. Heck!

Once again, the alarm rudely rang out whilst I was in the midst of deep sleep. My crew grunted. It was dark outside. Queenborough was our destination. We needed to be away and had three hours of ebb left to get down to the Spitway crossing.

The dawn rose in a suffused light, hinting very much of rain. It held off for some while, but we got a shower. I helmed whilst my crew, brimming with his infectious spirit, donned his full set. I, on the other hand, took my time putting bacon on the grill pan ready and preparing tea. Through the cabin window, I saw the squall dissipate, so only needed a jacket by the time I returned on deck!

We reached the Wallet Swatchway buoy in good time, crossing the shallow spitway near low water. "Head south…" were my instructions, as a Paul quizzically, studied the GPS map in front of him. "It'll be fine," I said, grinning. Soon after, we swept over the Whitaker Spit with a metre to spare and the bacon sizzling under the grill.

Munching our bacon sandwiches on a relatively good course down the Swin Channel, we spotted the *Cambria* coming away from anchor deep within the East Swin, an ancient bargemen's anchorage. The rain had left the atmosphere murky, hence our not spotting her earlier.

"Both bound for Queenborough," I said, "she's booked for the town's traditional craft event this weekend." And, almost as an afterthought, 'So is *Whimbrel*…'

We couldn't clear the Swin's foot without tacking, so, as the tide was rising, I used a swatchway through the Barrow Sand I'd sailed through the previous year, with another crew – a brother and our sister.

We tacked deep out towards the main shipping lane, then back to the Essex shore, west of Blacktail Spit. The *Cambria* had sailed to the Sheppey shore and ultimately managed to cheat the ebb's first flush and creep into the Medway. The barge fetched up along the northern mud line of Deadman's Island. Aboard *Whimbrel*, we finally resorted to our iron-topsail whilst working over the Grain Flats a little short of the gaunt old fort 'guarding' the river's entrance.

It was a bit of a grey passage, but we did feel a bit of sun at times. Quite different from the week of benign weather just enjoyed. But we'd had a passage breeze with a good sail to boot and happiness floated round our decks, which is always good.

Soon after mooring, we were sitting back over a pot of tea, nattering. The flow of words was suddenly disturbed from close by across the water. A startling piecing cacophony. "Birds…" my crew exclaimed. There, on the tide line, a frenetic squabble was taking place. Yes, the mudflats were alive here with numerous waders of varying species. But we'd both yawned several times. I was tired: the medication for my prostate cancer seemed to sap my energy, more often than not. Rest and sleep were needed. I slid below, whilst Paul lay back, head on cushions and was soon away…

I awoke to a dry throat. My crew was up and about and had quietly cleared our tea things. "Beer time," I said, grinning. "Did you sleep?" I received a double "Yeh," if one includes the head nod!

A beer was soon in hand, chuckling, I said, "What a grand place this is," taking a large sip of my beer.

"Wasn't so nice when the glue factory belched…" Paul quipped. But that was long ago when we were both very much younger. The town's dirty industries had all evaporated, one after the other. It probably left the town 'poorer' and a decline occurred, but slowly, slowly, times were changing for this quaintly delightful and underappreciated place. My mate and I loved it. I told Paul about my mate wanting to buy an old house up the high street. It was years ago…just sometimes a little tweak of sadness passes about not taking the plunge!

At our call, the friendly Queenborough 'liberty' boat ranged alongside and we sallied forth in pleasant conditions for a celebratory jar or two in the town's finest pub, the Admiral's Arm, where I enjoyed a pickled egg dropped into a bag of crisps, for good measure. Yum!

Once back aboard, after eating at a different hostelry, we did imbibe in a nightcap with our coffee, to end the evening.

Nearing 'home' sails are stowed...

Our last day dawned. Breakfasted and tidied we readied for the short sail – it was by the weeks average – across Sea Reach of the lower Thames. There was an hour of ebb left as we sailed off the buoy. Reaching outbound under a friendly south-westerly, Queenborough diminished insight and Paul's beloved Admiral's Arm remained a memory (he keeps in regular touch from across the other side of the globe).

An hour or so after low water we swept past Southend Pier, then the Leigh Buoy and skirted a recently laid set of buoys marking a hooked sandbank. Passing, I was pleased to see one corresponded to an input on my GPS map, made of the edge earlier in the year. We were in home waters.

As a finale, it was an enjoyable cracking sail up the Ray, hard on the wind and heeling well, the bow sent up intermittent showers of droplets that sparkled in the sunshine.

The boat was left ready: on the morrow, the week's end, Christobel and I were sailing off to Queenborough for the harbour's end of season traditional boat rally.

It was on our return to *Whimbrel* that I saw a note left by Paul in the logbook. I read his words: "Mission Achieved! Thanks, Nick, it was fun and I'll remember it for years to come…"

It is hoped he will: this Kiwi is a fine shipmate!

Yarn is a much fuller version of an article previously published in Yachting Monthly, July 2020 – Recapturing an East Coast Childhood.

13
Sailing into Spring...

The unwavering signs of spring were taking place in gardens and hedgerows as the long winter lockdown in England began to thaw during March of 2021. It had been particularly wet earlier in the lockdown period, resulting in seriously muddied walking conditions – even in Essex – but as time moved on the weather became almost balmy. The blackthorns became heady with their scented flowers as our venerable Government got schools back into 'the swing' without causing problems of any significance, and further rejoicing took place. The lack of a 'kick-back' silenced the 'doomsday philosophers' who had been peppering the media channels, driving sane human beings to distraction. For me, it meant the radio or television 'off' knob had been hit, quite often!

Towards the thaw, my own thoughts had all too easily 'fixated' with a supreme desire for an unfettered change to the rules and regulations. I needed a sail! But, as time progressed, it became clear that the doors to additional freedoms would be unbolted in line with 'the plan' laid out by 'our guardians' a month earlier, easing my mind.

The 'crack' in the doorway allowed people greater freedom of movement outdoors – for which I rejoiced. The eventual reopening of sports facilities, for outdoor activity, including golf was the signal sailors wanted to hear. For golf was synonymous with 'sailing' from a club.

So, for sailors with craft afloat, an opportunity to exercise upon the water was dangling tantalisingly in front of our eyes, swinging metronome-like, teasing taste buds desperate for the sea air afloat. The dying days of March held the moment. Strangely, open boats, canoes and paddleboards and such had been allowed as a means of exercise from a public beach or hard during the long winter, as was open water swimming! The sanction over cabined craft operated in the proscribed 'bubble' appeared to be nonsense...

At some point during the preceding weeks, I'd said, "Thank

goodness…we enjoyed that gorgeous sail on New Year's Day!" Christobel, bless her, had smiled and ruffled my hair. Looking at her, I was sure she was probably thinking nothing more than it needed another trim.

Our 'boy' sailing Whimbrel on New Year's Day 2021.

In accordance with good seaman-like common sense and the river authorities long-standing advice for boat moorings to be checked regularly, I'd been visiting *Whimbrel* routinely. I had been making use of weather and tide states to run the engine too.

Our main-stay occupation had been our daily walking, but we were both looking forward to being allowed to go further afield and refresh ourselves in pastures 'out of bounds' for so long. The drag, even though we kept busy, was beginning to affect us both, mentally. A restorative change was needed. Goodness, surely, our freedoms of movement will never be taken for granted in the future, until 'we' forget…

As that change approached, the weather had other ideas down in the eastern corner of England. The Thames estuary was enveloped in a line of gales that crept down from the north. Would they clear away? Would the 'first' day of sailing be scuppered? As I muttered to myself, unfortunately within hearing distance of my mate, my ears picked up a throw-back comment, "…no point in worrying about it…" she said, "you can still go down though…"

I wanted to say, "But you don't understand…" but that would have been stupid: she understands all too well!

The day of lockdown easing came. Yes, it was very windy! So, I slipped down to the boat and got on with a spot of sanding and varnish repair work instead. It was good for the soul. The wind was whipping up rollers out on the waters of Sea Reach with white breaking crests. Within my own creek, short steep wavelets danced across to the saltings and slapped under the boat's quarters. It was bright though with glorious sunshine. And indeed, the evening weather forecast for the next few days was good.

Christobel in silhouette, negotiates a 'shining' slippery pathway…

That next day floated in on a wave of warmth. A high pressure was dominating, bringing an airflow up from the deep south, Africa even, we were told by the forecaster. I shall remember the date for the rest of my life, I'm sure of that, Tuesday, March 30, highwater at just about 1400…

Over breakfast, Christobel asked, "What time do we leave?"

"Go straight after our walk," I said, adding, "be time to get ready and for another touch-up coat on some varnish repairs…"

"We can have that quiche for lunch then…" I nodded in response: I would be making up our lunch boxes after clearing breakfast!

We arrived at the boat with the tide creeping inexorably up the creek and gushing into the seemingly higgledy-piggledy rills running across the mud banks. It was glorious. The wind had abated to light south to south-easterly and the sun shone down gloriously. We soon had the sails readied and as the kettle heated, I added another coat of varnish to odd areas of deck and cabin side beading where coatings were under repair.

As soon as we cleared the mooring, Christobel took the helm briefly while I hoisted sail. Going back aft, I gazed aloft, my eyes callously passed quickly over the creases in the sails for they would take care of themselves. My gaze stopped, arresting on the contrasting colour of the deep blue sky encompassing us against the tan of our sails.

Christobel was leaning against the aft cabin bulkhead, elbows on the cabin top with both hands to her cheeks. I saw her lips pucker and her face flush. A hand lifted as she wiped a tear as it rolled down onto her cheek. As she replaced her hand, I said, gently, "I know," prodding her side tenderly, "…it's nice…" I felt utter relief too.

"Yes…" she said, turning with shining eyes and planting a kiss, before popping below to put the kettle on again. We sailed in a generally 'easterly' direction towards the Crowstone off Chalkwell, passing a seal hunting for its lunch. Off the beach, Christobel took over to helm along the shore towards the cockle sheds at leigh-on-Sea. I'd pre-booked a facetime call with my mother and we chatted as we slowly ran west. My mother who was ensconced in her care home in Wiltshire thoroughly enjoyed her sail too!

A number of dinghies were in the water and others preparing to launch from the yacht club racks scattered along the shore. It was great to see this activity – a safety boat from the 'Essex' was out, so some were probably being sailed by youngsters. Paddleboarders and canoes proliferated too and, believe it or not in the dying days of March, a handful of swimmers were partaking of the brine, but they're a hardy lot!

There had been media reports of 'personal watercraft' (PWC's) causing trouble on my river and other rivers and coastal waters round the country – even the Times newspaper had a leader about the problem. A report too on the likelihood of Government being pressurised to include such craft within rules governing shipping and boaters alike. It was something of a surprise: I'd always thought PWC's were considered a 'boat' which clearly, they currently were not! But to get to the point, we suffered several of these 'yob controlled' infernal machines coming up to our stern and racing close under the bow. It was disconcerting. It also left us rocking and rolling violently in the wash waves.

Later, off the Leigh-on-Sea waterfront, we witnessed gross stupidity: there were swimmers in the water, paddle boarders and people in canoes. A large group of PWC's raced in close to the shore doing 'wheelies' creating wash waves that were breaking over the seawall, soaking pedestrians. We heard later that those shenanigans apparently reached a point where a member of the public called the police. During the year of 'lockdown' the sales of PWC's had apparently rocketed as people found an outlet for spare cash and energy.

We crept up past the Belton Way Little Boat Club and almost sailed into the entrance to the Lower Thames Marina based at the old Johnson and Jago yard by the 'new' Leigh rail station.

"Start the engine…" I called as I came round, spotting that boats were moored to long fore and aft lines preventing passage through, "have to power clear of these…" It was but a couple of minutes and silence was returned as we tacked, lazily, eastward out of the tightish spot, passing two Finesse craft, a '24' and a '21' on the way.

Clearing the end of Two Tree Island, it was a straightforward reach out to the Ray Channel. As the hilly bulk of Leigh fell astern, our speed increased in a freshened breeze. As we passed close by the saltings, I could see Brents paddling amongst the previous season's cordgrass stalks. It would be two months before they'd fly off to the Russian arctic north to breed on the food-rich waters draining from the tundra.

Shaking myself out of a semi-distant feel, I saw we had travelled on quickly. "Okay," I said, "I'll drop the main and you can run in…" That was a signal for the mate to take the helm. Mainsail stowed and fenders rigged ready, we ran towards our creek with a breeze that had become decidedly more easterly. It had a chill too, reminding us of the nearness of winter's end.

'Drop it…' I called, and Whimbrel slipped into her berth…

Entering the creek and butting the first of the ebb, I could see a couple of bystanders, watching. One called out as we passed, "Nice day for it…"

I chuckled and waved back, heartedly, calling, "It was just fantastic to be out…"

Approaching our mooring, Christobel said, "Here you take her…" handing me the helm, she walked forward, pushing fenders overboard on the way and then stood at the mast by the jib hoist, ready to let it run.

Judging 'the moment' I called, "Now…" and the headsail fluttered to the deck, to be gathered and cleared to port, away from the mooring cleats. As we slid, cross tide, towards our mooring, Christobel was ready to grab and hold onto a post, whilst I brought the boat to a stop with the stern line. Good girl, nicely done!

Tidying the sails undercover and into a bag, I thought back to our last sail, on New Year's Day. It was nigh on three whole months before. Three months of a limited ability to do things. A limited ability to move far from home. It had been hard at times, but we'd made the best of it, in the worst of times, I knew that.

Yes, two days before, we had passed through the equinox into spring. It had me in its grip as we left *Whimbrel*, tidied and covered. I had a proverbial spring in my step, almost skipping back along the walkways to the shore.

Yes, our first post full lockdown sail. Goodness me, reaching our car, we both positively glowed with pleasure…

14
Puff, Pop, Bang, It Was Gone…

The ban on sailing or going out afloat aboard a cabined vessel be it a – sailing cruiser or motor vessel – was lifted as March 2021 petered out and April approached. I'd whooped with joy at passing this milestone, which when the use of other forms of small craft had been allowed, had felt a little onerous.

As luck would have it, the weather gods weren't listening to our government's statements, of 'you can go…'! On the very day of the announcement, there was an inclement weather pattern with a high wind blasting up and down the Thames estuary and beyond. On a visit to my creek, the Sea Reach of the Thames was turgid. Spume was visibly streaking freely from tumbling white crests. It was very a wild scene indeed. It wouldn't last long, surely…

I was metaphorically straining at the leash, desperate to get out and sail. As said elsewhere, the boat had sat, week after week, ready for that regular sail on the tide I'd become used to over so many years!

Patience, patience…my thoughts had kept on repeating, to appease my soul. Of course, we did get out the very next day, as previously written about.

As time passed, we enjoyed another sail out of the creek. Clearing the moorings, I looked to the south. It was just one of those things really, kind of natural, something I'd done for years. I was struck by something, initially unfathomable, so I got on with navigating our creek's buoys and headed where the wind dictated.

Looking beyond he boat, things still seemed fresh and as my gaze took in what normally was taken for granted, but I was struck by the distant Kent shore, again. "Something's missing…" I murmured without thought. "It's the chimney's…" I uttered, unintentionally aloud.

The mate looked at me with a quizzical countenance, before saying, "What?"

I said, "I was puzzled…" and pointing across the water, added,

"…the shore is devoid of our once familiar power station chimneys."

The mate said nothing and continued to enjoy the water, smiling.

Chuckling to myself and mouthing 'Silly boy…' for those chimneys had been demolished for several years. Interestingly, I mused, one's memory doesn't so soon dispatch into history things that were once common 'friends' known since childhood days. I miss them!

Apart from a group of short stubby affairs, there weren't any chimneys to look at anymore. When the oil-burning giant on the Isle of Grain was demolished, it became noticeable that a gas-powered generating station had risen close by. Why the goodness 'we' were consuming gas for electricity production continues to baffle me!

"Ah yes…" I mused, chuckling, "I attended the fall of both." I continued to smile in the recollection for I had enjoyed a couple of cracking overnight sails alone.

The first was the 'big' Isle of Grain chimney, but it was to the second, a lower affair, the Kingsnorth Power Station chimney my thoughts rested. For more years than I care to remember, it was a point to aim for when clearing the eastern end of Canvey Island's marsh point. The other used to be a marker for the Medway, from afar afield as Clacton, when coming down the Wallet and then the Swin passage.

"Do you remember…" I said to the mate, "when we sailed up into East Hoo Creek and dropped anchor?"

"Yes, a van came up onto the sea wall and followed us. Some men then sat and watched us a while…"

It was during a mass protest about the burning of coal and oil for electricity generation. Protesters had scaled the chimney and hung placards at the top of it. The power station wasn't generating at the time, but the boilers would have been kept warm by firing from time to time. The proverbial had hit the fan and police and security guards were all over the place, watching! Later we had sailed in close to the end of the coal jetty and vans had come at speed to the end…

"You should write about it…" the mate said, looking inquisitively at me as my mind began to digest the subject.

Yes, I had slipped away alone on an overnight sail towards the end of March 2018 to witness the destruction of the Kingsnorth

Power Station chimney. So, returning from that sail with my good shipmate, I decided it was time to write the little story down.

On local media and boating association sites, the imminent demise of the chimney was being advertised for March 22, 2018. As the day approached, I was scanning weather reports and forecasts. "Looks good," I said over breakfast the day before.

"Go then…"

"I intend to…"

"Shall I get some shopping for you?"

Grinning happily, I said, "No, I'll get anything needed on way down tomorrow…grab stuff from the freezer." All was agreed in a jiffy!

Departing the creek with a light to moderate westerly blowing, the jib was set for the run out over the flood. Clear of the creek's entrance I set the main and enjoyed a pleasant sail across to the River Medway.

It was not too cold, being in the region of ten degrees, but keeping warm was a priority and my ears still burned warmly from the 'lecture' from my good mate before leaving home!

Once ashore, a pint, crisps, and a pickled egg!

Crossing the sparkling waters of the London River, I gazed at the distant chimney. It stood erect, proud and purposeful looking. It was set against a blue sky. Many people 'love' chimneys. I'm not an ardent lover, but they do have an elegant beauty. At the wider base, the way an almost surreptitious curve leads to a slender rise into the sky is, to my mind, graceful. The fact that the top of any old chimney belched acid and poison for decades is another issue. Little did it know of its imminent demise, I thought, chuckling.

Closing the harbour at Queenborough I got no answer from my radio call, so, with copious moorings to choose from was soon securely moored just off the floating hammerhead. Although not late in the day, the afternoon was well advanced for the time of year, so after prepping a Bolognese sauce with good English sausages, I rowed the short distance and landed. The office was closed, as suspected for I'd seen no one about. My mooring fee was dropped into their honesty box with a note.

Ashore, I had a better view upriver across the top of the Tail Ness Saltings. The sun was setting sublimely on its last night…However, I quickly made my way to the warmth of an honest hostelry, The Admiral's Arm and refreshed myself with a pint or two with crisps and pickled eggs!

Later, with a flavoured coffee, a crescent moon shrouded in a milky haze reflected across the still surface of the West Swale off the Queenborough shore. It lit *Whimbrel's* deck adding magic to the moment.

Before I went below, a gentle breeze broke the stillness. Ripples, crisp, like a crunching of an apple, gently resonated on the ear, pinging against the boat's clinker lands. Downstream on reclaimed land, which was once the Lapwell Bank and a food rich mudflat for wading birds, the rotors of four wind turbines had begun to turn and a gentle thrum carried across the water. I mused, wind power has ousted oil and coal hereabout, removing the areas two major polluters.

Next morning, I was away a little after dawn, motoring in little wind. The bacon for a 'butty' grilled as I rounded Queenborough Spit to head west. Passing Deadmans Island and running along the mud edge mud, I watched curlews hunting for their own breakfast seemingly oblivious to the closeness of the boat's passage. Below, the narrow rind of fat was crisping on my bacon. Nipping below, I slipped it into a baguette to be enjoyed with a coffee.

The sky was streaked with grey high clouds against a sea-blue background. Passing the entrance to Stangate Creek, a summer haunt of many, it looked lonely. And then along Burntwick's tide riddled edges, I gazed briefly at the remnants of the 1980s' military buildings that against all odds remain standing. The chimney of the machinery house, I knew was in good condition. The barrack block, by then still visible across the saltings, had huge cracks in its walls caused by surges during spring tides. Ahead, obliquely, across those saltings, the doomed chimney awaited its fate. I soon left the manmade debris behind and was rapidly closing Sharp Ness.

The river had appreciably busied too. Large yachts went past under power, one with its helm clad in a long thick coat. Motorboats and RIBs full of people were in the mix. One RIB, black, with at least four black clad and helmeted bodies was clearly a police presence. A fast grey launch, sending up sheets of wash spray which sparkled in the sunshine, sped close by – to my annoyance – leaving *Whimbrel* 'rockin and rollin' in its wake. 'Bloody safety patrol, typical…' I mouthed none to happily in their direction.

When rounding Sharp Ness with its wall of hard clay washed smooth by the flow of tides, I always kind of marvel at the layering seen. It isn't flat either, the layers, stratus, have been inclined since they were laid down goodness knows how long ago. Possibly due to the easing of the 'south' downwards ever since the last ice age melted away. I noticed the ebb was slackening. A breeze filled in too and sail was set.

Good progress was made down Kethole Reach and on into Long Reach. After a couple of tacks, I was soon after in position close by the eastern end of the Kingsnorth Jetty, with 20 minutes to spare!

I sailed back and forth, clock watching, taking pictures, making notes and generally enjoying the buzz.

Surrounding the chimney's 'base' a myriad of vessels were collecting and anchoring like bees round honey. Upstream, more yachts, some under sail, were closing the western 'perimeter' being enforced by that speeding safety vessel.

Downstream, to the east, from where I had come, a lesser collection had quickly gathered. These would all be downwind – probably not the best of places for I knew from experience, a dust plume would follow.

The power station had been a Medway landmark since 1963 when it rose above the riverscape. I have, therefore, known it for all my life memory, as I had the bigger Isle of Grain affair. Coal ships were once a common sight for four decades. Then the effects of pollution and global warming began to become political hot potatoes and politicians ignored the science at their peril.

Thinking back to the decade of the 1980s and the numerous coal strikes and fights with government, it is awesome to now know that those years were the very last heady days of coal mining. Governments of both the leading political parties had been closing mines for several decades. By the time of the 'last big fight' the writing had been on the wall for many to see for years, but it was a sore process…

Time was running out for the poor old thing. She stood erect, proud (surely), awaiting her last 'smoke' set against a deep blue sky. Would she put up a good show, I wondered.

I tacked just before the anointed hour. As I came on a steady course, camera at the ready with a clear unobstructed view, I saw a puff, then heard a pop followed by a louder bang. Then, as if she had never stood on the river's shore, it was as if she'd never been there.

Down she comes…

As the plume of smoke and dust drifted east, the skyline was altered, yet again. Looking at notes made at the time, I'd written, "Change is perpetual, manmade or otherwise, but I was tinged with just a little sadness…"

I put the boat's head through the wind and ran with a decent westerly right on the transom towards Oakham Ness, homebound. It was an exhilarating sail down those widening reaches and out past the river's entrance, squeezed between Garrison Point on the Isle of Sheppey and the nose of the Isle of Grain. *Whimbrel* sluiced through the still early flood before reaching my point for working round the Grain Flats to head cross-tide over the Nore.

I was soon bounding across Sea Reach, heading for the Essex shore, in a glorious fashion. Passing Southend Pier well to the west I had a brisk tack up the Ray Channel with the flood lifting us along and soon found myself off Smallgains Creek. Sail was stowed and I motored in.

I'd soon be enjoying tea with my dear mate, at home…

An entry in *Whimbrel's* log reads: 'Puff, pop, bang, it was gone…'

Farewell, old friend.

15
An Overnight During
Our Second Covid Spring...

Another spring was dawning nicely, 'released' but with continuing restrictions as we set off for an overnight sail soon after it was allowed during the embryonic months of 2021. My thoughts turned to a year before when the whole of the United Kingdom and much of the wider world, were in some form of Covid-19 lockdown, until summer was well into its stride.

We had just been 'set free' after virtually three months of hard lockdown with a slight easing of another five weeks allowing our earlier sail on the tide during the day. We were now into the next level of easing, allowing overnight sailing, caravanning and camping, etc. Would this be for the last time? Would enough of the world's population be vaccinated a year hence? Would precautions still be needed, in one form or another? So many questions with possibly frightening answers to ponder upon.

Of course, I, like many people, had an expectation that some form of self-protection was highly likely, ongoing. All of that though was for our leaders to sort out, in all probability in conjunction with many other countries. Both the mate and I sincerely hoped that the levels would dwindle to at the most, perhaps, of a mask in busy places and perhaps inside shops. Time would tell, but for the moment we were free to sail away from home.

At the end of the first week of being freed to sail away from home in a household unit, the weather became settled with a generally northerly flow. The nights were cold, but by day we were enjoying fine sunshine from largely clear skies. The early part of the week had seen frosts most nights, with snow, yes, snow, in the southern half of Britain. It skirted the east coast of Essex, thank goodness!

"Yes, I'm happy…" Christobel said, "but in the afternoon please, not early morning…" I kind of knew that even before the question was broached, for it was on the tip of my tongue! We wanted to go because we could, it being allowed. It was also to get a first 'overnighter' of the year under our belts. It sets the season and helps greatly to take stock and list what's missing, like the comforting things one has – we hadn't dug the comfy cushions out of our loft at the time and I hadn't my down below slipper-shoes either!

The forecast was good. Essentially quiet, dry with cold nights. Warm outer garments were packed.

"Are you taking the dinghy?" Christobel asked on the day of departure. I nodded, as she added, "might get a little sail…" I thought it doubtful due to the timing of tides and such, but…

The tide wasn't until late afternoon, but we got organised and went down to our boat's mooring in good time to get organised. I put the dinghy at the foot of the club's hard ready for the first of the tide in the creek. It was quiet. Raising the burgee, it flicked back and forth languorously, showing a distinct lack of interest. "Can see us motoring across," I called to my mate, who was down below decks, stowing our stores. "What was that?" she asked, poking the headsail bags out of the fore hatch.

"We won't need the jib…" I said, pushing it back towards her, adding, "I'll rig the genoa only…" Christobel looked aloft, smiling knowingly!

We both quietly worked with our readying tasks, finishing them, I looked aft and saw the tide was rushing up the gulley astern of *Whimbrel's* mooring. "Time for a coffee…" I was asked. I nodded for it would be 20 minutes before I needed to walk round to the slipway to row the dinghy back. I mentally reminded myself not to forget the rowlocks. I forgot them once, but no matter, I sailed the dinghy down the creek!

Soon after coming back with our tender, the tide was threatening to lift *Whimbrel* from the mud womb in which she sat. The centre plate wire tensioned as the boat lifted with a whoosh of air being sucked into the box too.

"Right, we're afloat," I said, disturbing my mate's affair with a book! She jumped to it, lifejacket already on and held on by the mast shrouds as the last two lines were removed. A burst astern and we were clear…sails were set as soon as we cleared the mooring.

With the engine in neutral, we slowly reached out over the incoming flood. Clearing the moorings, it was clear the wind was fickle indeed. For a short while, we looked at Brents dabbling along the edges of the saltings and in amongst the banks of last year's cordgrass fronds. The fresh stalks were still to show clearly.

"Look…" I said quietly, pointing, "the terns…they're back." For me, that was a clear sign of spring and a sight that always gladdens the heart immensely.

Yes, once outside, what breeze we had, wasn't enough to make a reasonable passage speed, but I persevered for a while: it was just so lovely to be on our way. There clearly was a breeze along the Leigh-on-Sea and Chalkwell shores, but off the Canvey Point, little or nothing. Far in the distance, a little boat with reddish tan sails was moving smartly under the hills.

"Pass the glasses out please…" I called to Christobel who had gone below to make a coffee. Through the binoculars, I could see the craft's hull clearly. Light blue. "It's *Poppy*…" I said chuckling. The name *Poppy* belongs to a little Hunter 22-foot gunter rigged cutter, shallow draft with a centre plate. The owners once owned a Finesse in a boat share partnership.

Soon after passing the West Leigh Middle, it was clear that the tide was getting the better of us on our attempted sailing direction – we were slowly but perceptibly sliding upstream! The trusty old diesel beneath the cockpit sole was 'forced' into life and we continued, motor-sailing under main alone. After the days and days of wind that we had been 'enjoying' it was just so typical. Still, we were out, afloat, free with intent on enjoying the moment…

It is pretty 'boring' motor-sailing and I was soon taking as much interest in the panorama round us as we coursed across the tide of the ship channel where, latterly, I have more often than not used the engine to ensure being well clear of the buoyed deep-water section for ships the big modern ships come from both directions at speed. It isn't very wide, so a short burst is all that's needed! Clearing the channel, we headed obliquely into the flood passing the West Nore Sand and into the Jenkin Swatch, or Nore Channel as it is now better known these days. Interestingly, I've recently heard a tug master using the term when talking on the port radio channel.

The mate took over and I wandered the deck looking at various things. Aloft too, running my eyes along the rigging stays, halliards and up the run of the mast, satisfying myself that all looked well. Dropping below, I called, "Tea, coffee?" Hearing an affirmative, I put the kettle on.

Back on deck, I leant on the cabin top and gazed about. Above, a strange cloud pattern hung over us. They were mirrored on the water surface, where the light and shades were being broken by a little breeze ruffling the water's surface. For a short while, I was mesmerised. Awaking from my 'slumber in the arms of Morpheus' I realised that those ruffles were indeed a breeze worthy of use.

We were nearing the gaunt old fort at the Medway's entrance at Sheerness and with a slant from the east I hoisted the genoa, to enjoy a sail, at least, into the historic harbour and on into the West Swale.

We'd changed positions at some point and I was on the helm as we crept past the Queenborough Spit buoy off Swale Ness. "Call them up by the pylons…" I said, noticing the mate looking expectantly. The 'pylons' are two wooden structures marking the outward extent of the burnt and dismantled Queenborough steamer pier.

A mooring line and the boathook line had earlier been readied. We sailed into the harbour. 'Usual buoy…' was the response to our call to the harbour master.

Christobel went forward, ready. "That's the one," she called back to me, pointing. The headsail was dropped as we came round, almost on a reciprocal course. I jogged along playing the mainsheet to control our speed against the tide's flow. It was on the ebb, but still running into the Swale. The buoy was hooked and while the main slatted the mooring was made fast. That buoy, apparently, we've discovered, the harbour authorities affectionately call, 'ours'!

An early May boat feast that evening.

The kettle had hardly had time to boil and the harbour launch ranged alongside. The boatman having not seen us since the previous autumn had come over to say hello and give us a welcome. Christobel fed him a chunk of cake, much to his delight!

It was a nice feeling to be back in the north/south running stretch of water sitting off the ancient town of Queenborough. We didn't go ashore…we'd missed the pub being open! No matter, I had a bottle of beer or two under the floorboards, which I enjoyed whilst preparing grilled pork with roasted peppers lubricated with a drop or two of beer…

As we finished our supper, the setting sun was caught on the polished stainless-steel casing of our heater setting it 'a fire' mimicking the heater burner already, warming the cabin.

I stood awhile in the hatchway, watching the last of the setting sun and looking round the quietness of the harbour's evening. The tide, by then sluicing out towards the River Medway, had an oily look in the calm. Ashore, lights were beginning to twinkle in the gathering evening. It was towards the end of May, hard to believe that in less than a month, the longest day would have passed us by, yet summer was still to come…

The setting sun caught the heater's polished stainless surface.

Later, but not much later, we turned in, both tired for we'd done a 10-km walk in the morning too, before we departed to the boat. Lying on 'my side' of the forward bunk, I listened to the hand bell-like 'plink, plonk, plink…' of water gently lapping under the plank lands. It's a soporific sound and only happens when there is a calm with gentle movement. When windy, the noise is scrunch-like. A hand came across and squeezed mine – 'nice day…' – and sleep overtook both.

In the morning, we popped ashore to pay our dues and take a short brisk exercise walk. A takeaway coffee and a slice of cake were enjoyed from the recently opened Bosun Store Café. The place had lain empty of life for far too many years following the closure of a 'famous' chandlery business. Now though, it has been rejuvenated, structurally and visually, adding to the town's waterfront charm. A brave venture in the midst of what we were all currently going through. One could only wish them well, which we did. Be even better when able to relax over a pot at a table…

Back aboard we readied for an immediate departure to take the last of the ebb out of the River Medway. Our sails were set ready. As the mooring was dropped, *Whimbrel* forged ahead on a tack across to the harbour pontoon where staff waved in response to our departing salute.

Several tacks were needed to clear the West Swale in shifty conditions, the air flow settling once clear. I've become convinced that the four wind turbines alter the flow vectors across the waterway, especially when from the easterly quarter.

Christobel Two Hats!

Passing some coffee out I noticed with amusement my mate's fresh headgear and laughed uproariously! Underneath her usual hat, she had pulled on a balaclava. "I'm not getting cold…" she said defiantly. I was 'forced' to take a picture!

Recently arrived terns were feeding along the shallows and disturbed water flows across Queenborough Spit. It's always a glorious sight, seeing these birds for it heralded spring proper. The way they can hover, then dart-like, dive, to hit the surface before rising with a little silvery fish or shrimp between their beaks.

Later, out in the Thames channel, I watched as a couple of these birds rise from a channel buoy and follow the propeller churned wake of a passing ship, feeding as if their very life depended upon it – which of course was absolutely true. It was a blessed reminder that in the world's current turmoil deep within a pandemic, nature continued with such serene constancy.

Yes, we enjoyed our humdrum but delightful overnight sail, whetting the appetite for more.

16
A Covid-19 Sailing Year...

As I set off on my first sail of 2020, I, like many, was sublimely oblivious to what was developing in a far off, yet highly interconnected land. My mind was set, as usual, on gleaning as much use of *Whimbrel* as I could, whenever the weather allowed, during the bleakest of the winter's months.

The year had moved into its third week before a day dawned with a forecast conducive to winter sailing in daylight. It was a glorious one too and spirits were lifted over the breakfast table.

Sailing out of my creek on the mid-afternoon tide, I marvelled at the sparkling sunshine slashing a rippled surface as it was brushed by a south-westerly breeze. I felt elated. The jib, hoisted off the mooring, was pulling meaningfully and the boat ran out over the flood with a chuckle from the clinker plank lands.

Clear of the creek, the main was hoisted. "That's better," I said, sighing deeply. It was a breeze strong enough to give *Whimbrel* a bit of a heel. From the bow, a clear rustling lifted to my ears as the bow cut the water. It felt wonderful.

I fetched along Hadleigh Ray and up Benfleet Creek. It was a close haul most of the way to below the Benfleet tidal barrier beyond the Island's other yacht club – a regular route at the time. The run back over the tide was glorious. It was good to be out on the water, alone, but I was missing my good mate: she was otherwise engaged and would have loved it too.

As the sun began to dip to the horizon, sails were stowed under the saltings edge clear of Smallgains Creek and the trusty diesel was fired up for the short passage in. It was sublime sail...The creek had a languid 'oily' look in the quiet of the gathering evening. The colours were awesome.

It was nearly a month before my next sail. It was even more pleasurable because my dear mate was aboard. It was an early morning sail. The sun had just come above the eastern horizon, spreading its new born colours across the Thames stream. While I got busy with 'preparing for sea' Christobel got our breakfast bacon under the grill, a job of the greatest of importance; the result was yummy! Thankfully, it was an equally sublime sail. No stress, just pure joy.

Local walking in lockdown – the Hadleigh downs, looking over Leigh-on-Sea.

But as the new decade came into sharper focus during the end of January, no one, apart from perhaps a few souls within the world of epidemiology envisaged what was soon to hit Europe and in particular the British Isles. A small news item from the city of Wuhan in central China during the early days of the year was about to grow into a megalithic media circus.

The term 'corona virus' was well known amongst scientists for there have been many strains over the years, most of huge insignificance. The common cold is a variety. Now though, anyone above the age of about four years old will be familiar with it as Covid-19. During the weeks before Christmas 2019, the disease was unknowingly on the rampage. Its 'toxicity' was unknown too. Before long, countries round the globe were reporting people sick, extremely sick indeed. People began to die from something seemingly untreatable. A pandemic of tsunami proportions was declared, as it raged across the world. The official designation given to the disease by the World Health Organisation was Sars-CoV-2.

Very few people had taken much notice then, but we were soon to discover that the disease had an unexpected severe and acute effect on the respiratory system and other problems akin to kidney disease.

As time passed a significant number of survivors were found to be so traumatised, breathing and limb use was found difficult. This was given the name 'Long Covid' but thankfully most people responded to therapies. Initially, medics round the world were trying a whole raft of drugs used for other treatments. Amazingly, a large number were found to act positively against the effects of the disease and reduce fatalities. But they weren't a cure or vaccine.

Traditionally, my younger brother has been invited for a sail over a weekend close to his birthday during the early part of March. We have often sat out in the cockpit, enjoying a post supper coffee with frost building on the deck round us. Warmly wrapped, it's never concerned us! The forecast during the run up was so bad that neither of us thought we'd succeed; however, the weather gods produced a 'window of opportunity' and we willingly grabbed it!

So, two weeks before the 'fated' National broadcast from our esteemed Prime Minister, we had an overnight dash to Queenborough and back. Neither of us had any inkling that it would be my last sail for over two months and that he would be the only family member who was able to enjoy a sail aboard *Whimbrel* during that first Covid year.

As we all found out, during the epidemic, various forms of restrictive rules were applied throughout. For a large part of the first year of lockdowns and partial periods, our son, who lived alone, was excluded from 'coming in' but later 'lockdowns' allowed single occupants to form a 'support bubble' to alleviate mental stress. It was a lesson learnt, but it was too late for many people.

Towards the end of March 2020, as the epidemic was reaching a crisis point regarding what direction our government would take, with thoughts of 'herd immunity' against full lockdowns, and a long diatribe against 'bringing down the shutters' from the chattering classes, *Whimbrel* was lifted from the water. We changed the centre plate lifting wire before she was chocked up, positioned well away from other craft. It was out on 'an exposed edge' for a contractor to remove the bottom paintwork using a slurry blast 'wash' which did not eat into the wood planking. That done, she was left to dry. It was our initial intention to go away for a few days, however, I had already moved the booking to the autumn, as a precaution.

The same weekend, we made our last trip to London by train for over a year to collect a picture we had purchased at an exhibition by the Wapping Group of Artists. It was sobering trip, for even then, many people had taken to wearing masks over mouths and noses. Lockdown or at the very least, a form of restrictive measures was coming, we both thought.

The National Lockdown came upon us like a ton of bricks squashing all and sundry. I immediately began considering the damage to the boat's bottom. After thinking about her predicament, with an unpainted bare wood bottom, we got on and finished the job, maintaining our bubble. It could not be left in that state for long without causing severe damage.

The other problem was that the boat was in a temporary storage spot, purposely out of the way for the blasting. The ground was 'soft' and her chocks were continually working loose in the regular periods of high winds. So, as the boat was originally to be moved to a different storage/working spot, the understanding club hierarchy allowed her to be put back into the water. The activity was a 'family affair' not affecting others. Our insurance company, who were aware of our boat's 'journey' ashore was greatly relieved she was safe in her mud berth, rather than ashore.

From friends of wooden boats at other yards, I heard thirdhand news of their craft being put back into the water for better care. The extreme drying out of a wooden boat is something to be avoided, even in 'normal' times! In the southern half of Britain and in the east, particularly, it was a very dry and warm spring and two friends who had the same class of boat found that their vessels suffered from drying out more than was usual, but not severely, fortunately. They both went into the water at the earliest opportunity though, with one owner having to pump for several hours, returning during the night too, he told me!

We settled into a routine of daily walks of varying lengths. Less for cleaning day, none on shopping day. It wasn't long before a 'fatigue' set in of continually walking locally! We were used to going further afield, but it wasn't allowed…There was an enjoyable side for nature seemed to be more active against a less urgent human world. The songs within the woods surrounding our home were sharper. Out in the open, skylarks serenaded our way in a sky devoid of most jet engine noises.

Early on, during the first lockdown, we had stopped listening to my 'beloved' BBC Radio 4 morning programme. We were driven away for it had become nothing more than a continuous diatribe of vitriol and senseless cross-questioning. The action was followed for any television news too. We took to settling with a pot of tea for me and coffee for my treasure and composed ourselves for the evening 'update broadcast' and as soon as the first reporter uttered their first words, it went off. In that way, I'm sure we remained sane!

There were a few local people we soon began to 'keep an eye on' for one was essentially imprisoned. From afar, we could see my mother deteriorating too, living alone in her warden flat. A sister made covid secure visits, but even with carers several times a day, it wasn't enough and like many my ol' ma was diagnosed with what became known as 'Covid Syndrome' – brought about by a lack of quality human contact. Eventually, it came to a head and she ended up in hospital from where 'the family' decided she needed to be cared for 24/7. For an 'old Essex Girl' who loved the outdoors and getting afloat on her once regular visits to us in Essex, I could only feel a deep sadness. I'm sure my siblings felt it too.

Sadly, my mother died during the pandemic at the age of 90 and 12 days. It was early on Boxing Day 2021 our telephone jangled – my sister alerting her siblings. We 'dashed' from Essex, a brother from Cambridgeshire, neither of us making it. The eldest in Canada, couldn't, but he'd made a visit during the relatively clear autumn, for which he was thankful. My mother, like other elderly folk, essentially 'gave up' and slowly slipped away leaving the strange world peacefully.

There were many extremely sad tales through this period. My thoughts always went out to them, as I'm sure hundreds of thousands of other thought waves did too. Bless them.

There were a few things I had to deal with on *Whimbrel* and items were retrieved when carrying out weekly inspections of the boat's moorings. Other jobs were progressed too. One little affair was sorting out the plug and socket for the boat's navigation compass illumination lamp. New bits were ordered, online and a socket base was made from 'scrap' mahogany. I even had a spare 12-volt battery, so it could be tested before fitting! My crews are always hungry for more and more charging facilities aboard, so I also got hold of a multi-USB outlet and mounted it in another piece of mahogany. During that period, our conservatory spent time as 'my varnishing room' ousting all due to the fumes!

Then one morning, I said to my mate, "I'm thinking of making a wooden seat and lid for the loo…"

"Right…" was her response. Christobel knew that our 'so called' wooden seat and lid were in fact compressed paper which had begun to fail quite quickly in the atmospheric moistness found afloat.

"Got that big sheet of plywood in the shed…" It was the right thickness.

"What about splinters?" she asked quickly, squirming a little on her breakfast stool.

"It'll be epoxy coated…" I said, feeling slightly aggrieved. I wasn't sure of her return and added, "I'm sure it'll work…"

So, I spent a morning online and ordered epoxy, brushes and a jigsaw! Meanwhile, awaiting delivery of my orders, the boat's loo seat set was brought home and dismantled.

In glorious weather I made a lockdown loo seat for the boat!

Oh, what excitement I exuded on the day everything needed had arrived. I'd never used a jigsaw before so after drawing round the old seat parts, I had a few practise cuts before attacking the shapes in anger.

The weather was so glorious during that Lockdown April the garden became my open-air workshop. The cutting was easy. The shaping, with my trusty old spokeshave, was soothing, however, once the hand sanding bit was reached, perspiration rained from my forehead through my lops of unkempt hair. That hair was soon to be 'attacked' by my marital barber.

Over a year on, I'm very proud of my 'Covid-19 Lockdown Loo Seat' and it looks exceptionally good on the boat's loo. My regular crews got their chance to see it as the pandemic eased, but not defeated, during the sweet summer of 2021.

Alongside all those home jobs, as an easing took place during the spring we attacked the maintenance of varnish work aboard *Whimbrel* – something that was mainly my responsibility. Over a couple of fine days, Christobel beavered away hard sanding the main cabin tops ready for deck paint recoating. A job she so loves!

Cafés were allowed to sell takeaways … we took to an occasional picnic lunch with a glass of wine…

The foreshore world generally seemed to have a rejuvenated feel about it when sailing 'for exercise' was allowed once again during the middle of May 2020. Listening to the 'broadcasts' and reading the detail of the regulations, it soon became obvious that when golf was allowed, so was sailing (Later, boating was given greater explanatory detail, due, I believe, to transgressions). Going away overnight was clearly forbidden. This covered caravan owners and second homes too, to the annoyance of some – remember the 'near-riot' down west when campers and caravaners pitched up in a locale? The local residents went ballistic, demanding police action!

We enjoyed many sails out on the tide during the continuing exceptionally fine spell of weather. Looking back, the weather pattern, in the eastern area of England especially, seemed to have been so settled during those long months of lockdown restrictions that we were almost taking it for granted. It certainly made life that much more bearable. Elsewhere, however, there were many throughout the kingdom who did not fare so well. Floods were experienced badly in parts of England especially before the lockdown and in the immediate aftermath. Discussing this and more, we both felt for the thousands limited to 'street walking' in built-up areas.

On a fine Saturday in late May, we took the opportunity to use two tides in the day for a grand whole day sail. Clearing the mooring we hoisted sail and reached out of the creek, while below breakfast was sizzling under the grill. I feel there is something about the aromas given off when grilling bacon. Senses are tingled as something timeless and ingrained from childhood is awakened in my soul…

Munching and chatting, we sailed in a generally eastward direction letting the boat go where she was happy. It was a clear, slightly hazy day with a sun promising much more. And yes, the morning's crispness soon gave way to a spring warmth. Down near the West Shoebury buoy, off Southend-on-Sea, we passed some 'friendly' boats on a reciprocal course, enjoying a day out too and 'traded' the traditional waves of fellow sailors.

As the tide began to drop away, we turned back towards the Ray Channel, where close by our creek I put us aground on a sand patch. I had a job to do. The two sheer strakes were then rubbed down and varnished. Nearing the last few brush strokes, I was 'racing' the fresh flood as it crept up my shins then over my knees towards the bottom of my shorts. It was a good job done though and we had a fabulous day in the bargain.

I noticed about this time various 'boasts' on social media and 'yotty' blog sites were surfacing round the bazaars showing pictures of groups of automated identification numbers (AIS) of boats away from home overnight, anchored in creeks. The Kent Police, apparently, 'raided' Queenborough Harbour, over on the Isle of Sheppey. They wanted to know details of boats out but went away for it was clear the harbour had no control. I began to watch this media whirl but did not comment on anything I saw…the rights and wrongs were immaterial. Personally, we did what the regulations allowed…overnight sailing was not, so we didn't go. I even had a friendly chat to a chap I knew, returning with his wife after a bank holiday away sailing. We passed them during a sail out on the tide. The chap boasted somewhat. We were both aghast: he was an ex-commodore of a local yacht club. However, I couldn't see what real harm there was in it though!

Eventually, I wrote a blog on my website, referring to the conversation, asking 'yotties' nicely not to follow the antics of a certain Mr Cummings (a well-documented 'law breaker' and cause-celeb). As time went on, according to many senior Members of Parliament, it was stated that he was the direct cause for the rot that soon followed his indiscretions. The media made sure it became public knowledge. And soon academics referred to this as the 'Cummings effect' – indeed. I blithely considered that I'd made a point and thought, that was it!

(Note: a little over a year later, on May 26, 2021, Mr Cummings, sat before a Parliamentary Select Committee – he'd been sacked by the Prime Minister as his key adviser late in 2020. During his questioning, Mr Cummings apologised for his action in making a '100-mile' trip to test his eyes. To my mind the distance was immaterial, for it was far from local – many media outlets had figures of up 260 miles for the round trip. In his statement, Mr Cummings stated that it led directly to a breakdown in [some of] the public's adherence to the law. This struck a chord in my heart, in the light of what my mate and I were subsequently put through.

Of course, greater 'crimes' were going on within the offices of No. 10 Downing Street – up and down the country too if the truth was known. Of that, I'll say nothing other than I did eventually write to Prime Minister and my Member of Parliament about two people's sad and frightening experiences. Neither elicited a response, initially! My MP did eventually reply, offering help to reraise with police if desired … I declined for I have no wish to go through it all again.

Additionally, a public inquiry headed by Baroness Hallett has been set for 2023. She has included, quote, 'legislative and regulatory control, and enforcement' as an area to investigate due to many publicised problems associated with non-adherence. Hallelujah!)

"Got the dinghy to do next week…" I said, while we discussed the shopping for the coming week, after our long 'Thursday' walk.

"We'll do shorter walks for a couple of days," my mate said, helpfully. I had varnishing and the dinghy bottom antifouling coating to do. "Need any help?" she added after what seemed a long time. I shook my head, closing the conversation. Of course, all was done!

My sixty-fifth birthday loomed large too! It would be a quiet affair indeed, just the two of us, and the event wasn't celebrated properly until able to go for a champagne infused meal with 'the boy' sharing it with us too.

As a treat and in lieu of our not being away sailing during my birthday period – something which had become a fixture in our diary – the tides were right for another whole day sail. It was on a glorious Saturday and we cleared our mooring early for a sail across the Thames and into the River Medway. We had 12 hours of playtime…

Once allowed afloat, the water was filled by boaters, paddleboarders and picnickers too!

Boy, it felt great passing the gaunt old fort 'guarding' the River Medway's entrance, opposite Sheerness. We set a course inside of it, something done frequently when hitting that spot near or towards highwater, thus keeping out of any ebb that might be flowing.

We sailed inward until near Stangate Creek before turning. We then 'chased' a group of yachts from the Lower Halstow Yacht Club enjoying a club cruiser race. It was a great romp, out past the wreck of the Liberty Ship *Richard Montgomery*, before turning towards home, across the run of the River Thames.

We anchored along the Ray bank off Chalkwell, a favoured spot. I was ashore on the sands when I saw a chap walking towards me – from one of the 'friendly' boats seen on our previous day-sail a couple of weeks before. "Boat's going well…" he said, as an opener, before adding, "by the way, I think you're right…"

"What about?" I asked, naively, for I was about to learn of something very nasty indeed.

"What you wrote…" the chap said, grimacing somewhat. He clearly knew something…for he added, "He's wrong though…" Nothing further was elicited for whatever it was, I clearly didn't seem to know. It wasn't the case for long though: an evilness had surfaced from within the yachting fraternity along our shore.

News, by way of numerous third-party persons – good friends some of them – of a publicly stated threat to burn *Whimbrel*. It was made by the chap I spoke to out on the water who'd glibly boasted about flouting the regulations (law). I was particularly shocked: he was someone I previously had great respect for. My crime? I was accused of reporting him to the police.

I later learnt that following a 'club run' made by members of the man's yacht club, the Marine Police visited the club wanting to speak to some boat owners who had been away from home over a weekend. The chap that boasted to me was one of them. It was blatantly obvious, public boasts on 'yotty' chat sites and vessel AIS (automated identification signal) plots gave all the information needed, plus the fact that craft movements can be and probably were monitored by the river authority. Some authorities were chasing craft home at the time!

So, without naming any person or anyone's boat or club, I was blamed!

We'd laughed at first, not taking it seriously. However, after meeting some people at a yard in Leigh-on-Sea when the seriousness of the threat was forcefully reiterated to me. I felt it was of real serious intent and we were advised that it should be reported to the authorities.

I will not go into details, but suffice to say, it was reported – twice: Essex Constabulary 'lost' my first report! Then, after a later vociferous verbal assault that summer of 2020 whilst afloat, the police acted. The perpetrator later denied the assault but was 'warned' about any further reports of harassment being made and of consequences. I was not satisfied.

The verbal assault made while afloat would surely contravene the Merchant Shipping Act. It left us both severely traumatised. It took several hours for Christobel to become 'calm' and she later 'forbade' me to take my sailing tender out of her sight. I know now what I should have done. I should have put out a call to the Coast Guard asking for the police to attend us upon arrival at a safe haven.

Both of us realise this now with the progress of time. It was a hard lesson. The man who made the threat knows what he did, as does his wife, and his yacht club who admitted it to us, and many others up and down the shoreline. I kept my counsel, publicly, in not naming him, dear reader, but I would dearly, dearly love to do so.

When the case was closed by the police, several questions continued to float round my mind, often in the dead of night. Disturbed nights are fading as time moves forward, but a year or so on, a rawness often breaks the surface. Its stings will continue to plague for many years to come, I fear. It has changed both of our attitudes to our fellow sailors, for sure.

Back to those questions:

Did I feel released from the threat? No.

Was I honestly satisfied by the response of my local constabulary? No.

Did I feel safe on the water, going forward? No.

Did I feel fearful of the future? Yes.

This was all borne out in 2021, for wherever we went, Christobel and I scoured the moorings looking for our harasser, as our lives continued to be clouded as unwitting 'casualties' to the Covid-19 crisis.

As the sailing season progressed, we made sure we kept clear of yachts from our harasser's club. I did meet one couple on a marina pontoon in North Essex during our travels and we chatted for they had been supportive, but I purposely did not raise the incidents.

Later during that summer though, at a traditional boat festival, we attended at Queenborough, we were visited by a couple, who I suddenly realised were from the club in question. Christobel, who straight away showed them below, was blissfully unaware which I wanted for she was still reacting 'badly' to the mere presence of such people unless she knew them. It is said that time is a great healer, I hope so.

During the pandemic, social media outlets became a hugely dangerous minefield. Initially, I'd not noticed, but when the attacking threat was made, I went public. It was made abundantly clear by the mindless minority that as I had stuck my head above the parapet, I was fodder for vitriol. I was 'gunned down' in a merciless fashion. I learnt an enormously powerful lesson. Suffice to say, my spiritual feeling towards the 'yachting world' suffered severely. I wasn't expecting it. As time has passed, sadly, I've felt less inclined towards my fellows!

It was during the seemingly long and essentially pointless 'no going away' period, we also went to the help of a yacht that had gone onto a mud bank. She was from the same yacht club from where 'the threat' emanated, I soon discovered.

We had sailed east in a gorgeous slightly offshore north-westerly breeze and were reaching back up into Hadleigh Ray between the saltings lining the shores of Canvey Island and Two tree Island. I spotted a yacht heading towards where I knew mud lay in wait. I commented to the mate, "She's over the shallows…"

"Yes…so I see…"

I luffed up as a shout from the yacht drifted across the short gap, "Can you help…"

"Okay," I called back, "I need to stow sails first…" We cleared the danger area, luffed up and quickly stowed our canvas.

I turned back under power. On the way, I rapidly joined lengths of mooring warp to make a long towline. Ranging close by, I threw a coil…they dropped it. I retrieved it and threw again. It was got hold of but there then seemed to be some confusion aboard the little ship on how to run the rope and tie it off…

Below by then, Christobel called the port authority to alert them to the situation. Unknowingly to us, the call was heard by our own club's workboat.

We tried fruitlessly for what seemed ages, but was merely

minutes, to tow the stricken yacht clear. The tide was falling fast. It was no go! Then, I saw the workboat and, fortuitously, a passing RIB. I asked the RIB to transfer the tow to her. Thanks, chaps: they were short of fuel, they told us, but helped, nonetheless. Out on the water, most people do!

However, the workboat also failed in a further attempt to free the vessel. Being of a deep bilge keel design, she was well and truly hard aground. Unfortunately, our warps were subsequently dropped off by the workboat for the stranded ship to retrieve. I couldn't go near due to the depth, but as we left them, I made it clear what boat we were, my name and where we moored. I also advised them to let the local lifeboat station know...

The loss of our warps was a risk I took when going to help another. Christobel wrote to the yacht club. Nothing came of it. Those warps weren't returned to us, nor were there any thanks from the vessel's owner. A year on the situation remained in limbo. And after two years, it's clear they'll never be returned!

At the time, all I had aboard *Whimbrel* was my heavy 'Thames' mooring line, a couple of mooring lines used for mooring buoys and two other short lines. With cruising soon to be allowed, we needed warps quickly. A coil of rope was ordered online and once received a few days later, I made up four new lengths with spliced eyes in one end.

Some would have sailed on past, but that has never been our way. But, for some, it was clearly something given little thought. I starkly witnessed this a few weeks later when I saw a yacht's mast 'tumble' down. It had splintered and fractured at the hounds. Numerous boats, closer than I, aboard *Whimbrel*, went on past, seemingly without a care. Sailing to their position, I hailed the crew. They were content with their lot. The propeller was clear, they assured me. So, as I left them, I called, "I'll keep a watch..." With cheery waves and with the broken mast top and boom secured, they soon set off, motoring towards their Leigh-on-Sea foreshore mooring.

One of the joys that many found and it was certainly the case within 'the *Whimbrel* household' was more time for reading. I had a reasonable pile, topped up by that sixty-fifth birthday. My mate had always been a 'devourer' of books but had long finished reading her pile of library books. Every few days, she was to be seen 'ranging' her shelves of books…

Then, as if a miracle, the gloom of the land was lifted into far off clouds. We were released. Well, certain strings were attached, but for sailors it meant the rivers and creeks were available to us for holiday sailing. At the beginning of July of that first year, we could go away overnight.

Way back in the early spring we had organised a group trip with the owners of two other Finesse 24s with a meet up at Queenborough and Chatham in the itinerary. The original plan was for a visit to Conyer, but sadly the local marina was remaining closed to visitors for the summer. We agreed to meet the two boats at Queenborough, departing a day earlier. We went the 'long way' and sailed east to Harty Ferry for a night under the island's high hill. It was a fast passage through the 'inland' route to the Columbine, three nautical miles beyond Shell Ness, before we turned west, inside the Isle of Sheppey.

After anchoring off the old hard the wind-over-tide situation made it a horrible anchorage. So, we hauled our anchor and moved further west to the pool off Elmely Island where we enjoyed a tranquil late afternoon and evening. The following day we met the other two boats in Queenborough. The three of us looked splendid grouped on a buoy off the harbour's all tide pontoon. During the afternoon, Christobel enjoyed one of several 'epic' rows she made in *Twitch* during the summer.

It was great sailing in company upriver to Chatham the next morning. A convivial 'distanced meet' of the six of us was held round the decks of one vessel, before separating for our evening meals alone! The evening's sunset reflections within the marina were stupendous too.

Our club's fleet of Finesse 24s enjoyed a mini meet on the river Medway.

Leaving, it was a bit of a race downriver before we peeled away for a night in Sharfleet Creek. During our time away we returned to Elmley Ferry anchorage and enjoyed a walk ashore (written about separately).

"I've ordered some new chain…" I said one afternoon.

"Right…"

"How do you feel about a trip to Woodbridge for lunch?"

My mate looked at me with one of those looks known only to men, then grinned, saying, "By car…I assume." I nodded.

Later, following an email communication posted into my 'letter box' it was all arranged.

So, after picking up *Whimbrel's* thirty metres of galvanised chain and a joining shackle, we went on to Woodbridge. We didn't stop for lunch because the town was still essentially largely shut down! It was strange waking the usually busy main street. It was devoid of people. There wasn't the lively buzz associated with the town. It was sad. It was, like many places, a victim of Covid-19 too. Fortunately, we managed to find a café open, serving refreshments.

Peeling off the road home after crossing the Orwell Bridge, we dropped down to a local 'farm shop' we knew of and picked up the makings of a very pleasant picnic! Sitting in glorious sunshine, munching, we both longed to be aboard one of the many yachts seen sailing along the tranquil looking river. 'Preferably *Whimbrel*' I remarked, laughing.

Our plans, so materially changed, as they were too for so many countless millions, we decided to remain 'down south' enjoying the Medway, Swale and Thames, with a trip up to London for our summer sailing.

Wherever we went, we voyaged slowly, taking our time with stops at many places. Walking when ashore cost nothing and did us good. It kept us clear of other people and we 'reached into' the interior of our ports of call more than we usually did.

The highlight was our 'dawdle' up the River Thames to Limehouse, where I'd provisionally booked a berth during the spring. Departing from Queenborough, we stopped at the Gravesend Town pier's pontoon, where I met an old 'chum' from my boyhood days in Kent. A couple of hours were spent wandering the waterfront too. Fascinating.

When passing along the Mucking Flats sailing towards Gravesend, I remarked to my mate that it was two years since I'd made 'that call' to my contact a Southend Hospital indicating my chosen treatment route. Gloriously, another month onward, I was to cease that medication too. I have to say, my eyes moistened, just a little.

Departing, we enjoyed a glorious sail up to Dartford Creek, waiting for a short spell at anchor, before taking the tide up to Crayford's Dugdale Wharf to berth ahead of the spritsail barge *Decima*. We had to motor in due to wind direction, sadly.

The tide being late on the next day allowed us an enjoyable walk downstream and then inland past an ancient, moated establishment that had once been a Royal property with a creek-side wharf. On the long trek back along a busy road we found a caravan café open, serving decent coffee.

Moments after departure, the jib was hoisted, followed by the mainsail. As the effects of the land wore off, the wind increased and was blustery. *Whimbrel* shouldered aside the strong inward tidal flow in the narrow reed-fringed creek. It was grand. We were shadowed by a creek boat manned by a member of the trust looking after the interests of the two creeks – the chap later sent me a raft of photographs. Later, we moored, by prior arrangement at the Erith Yacht Club – a friendly and comfortable place. We didn't go ashore. There wasn't a need.

Our last stop before London was Greenwich. We love it there, but wished it wasn't so far into the old part by the old naval college. But there are still odd little enclaves of 'old' in amongst the modern on the peninsular. One gem sits on River Way, not far from the Greenwich Yacht Club. There is an old pub, recently renovated on our visit, and a pretty row of terraced houses.

We had a fabulous time at Limehouse. The clubhouse of the Cruising Association had tables to book, but we did cook aboard too. We met family members living in London and my cousin came up to town with his wife for a convivial evening. We love them all and appreciate their company. During our stay, we walked through many parts of a very empty London. It was a strange feeling. Walking across the square outside the Tower of London, we passed just three people…walking up King Street towards the Guildhall, we passed just one person. Normally it throngs with a heaving mass of contra-flowing bodies!

By the end of summer, 'we seemed to be floating clear' but there was a whispering in the breeze…I felt in my bones that we were in for a second peak. Too many people were not distancing, not keeping apart. The government and media kept saying 'how good everyone was…' No, they weren't, otherwise we'd have avoided the worst of what soon hit.

A bright spot was doing a spot of filming with BBC Southeast Today. A special reports producer wanted to film the grave of Royal Navy Surgeon, Sidney Bernard, who died of Yellow Fever aboard his ship while she was in quarantine in Stangate Creek during 1845. He was buried on Burntwick Island, then a sheep farm. I sailed over to Queenborough the day before to be ready to pick up the presenter and film/sound recordist. Welcoming them aboard the next day I got the presenter to sail the boat – he was chuffed. The camera/recordist wanted various off boat shots (lots of messing about!) and I nearly missed the right state of tide. Finally I took them into the saltings in *Twitch*. The tide was creeping upwards fast and was in the saltings when we eventually departed. I asked for care with camera shots for few people know of the grave's actual site! After dropping them back into Queenborough, I hightailed home to moor off my creek, to await the tide. It was fun…

The mate and I had a 'cottage' holiday based at a working mill in Boston, Lincolnshire and the delayed holiday in the delightful town of Deal. Early in March, I'd had the foresight rebook this one for late October. The world, it was said by many, would be free by then. What did they know: a week after our return, England went into another lockdown, phew!

During that autumn lockdown, interestingly, sailing for exercise was allowed. Although tidal jaunts were permissible, due to weather conditions I only got out once aboard *Whimbrel*. Such is life! We did enjoy a long-promised sail on the newly built spritsail barge, *Blue Mermaid*, operating within Covid regulations for ships, which was fantastic (written about).

As the culmination of the year approached, a great debate about a 'lost Christmas' took place. How can you lose Christmas? Christmas is a religious festival celebrating the birth of Christ. So, wherever one is, as a Christian, you can celebrate Christmas – or was I missing something? But of far greater importance than the raging arguments and tear-jerking of people saying 'it won't be the same' there was the 'small' matter of rising death rates, infection rates and the weariness of the medical experts warning of an approaching second wave. The only news worth hearing was of the first two vaccines, both developed in record-breaking time. More were on their way; we were boldly told. One overriding fact remained: No one would be safe until the whole world was vaccinated…

The mate and I saw out the year with a sail on the last day and we welcomed 2021 in the same fashion. Our 'boy' was able to sail with us and we enjoyed a New Year's Day breakfast of bacon and black pudding baps whilst under sail. It was rather chilly but the sun shone down on us as we clipped through the estuary waters. It was to be our last sail aboard *Whimbrel* for three long months…

With a staggering vengeance, the pandemic was re-released by too many fellow human beings ignoring advice, the regulations and a disregard of common sense. The experts kept warning us. Hospitals began filling at a remarkably fast rate, then, as if on cue, sadly, so did deaths. Putting it bluntly, the very worst was happening round us. The pandemic began to mirror the world-wide pandemic of Spanish Flue that followed in the aftermath of the first world war, a hundred years earlier. Sadly, the human species is slow to learn.

That was it. Three months of lockdown in England was decreed. It was during this period I 'suffered' my third lockdown hair trim. In my attempts to capture a 'selfie' my dear wife snipped an ear. It was just a scratch, but I got the all-important pictures, of spilt blood!

During all the various levels of lockdown, we did our utmost to keep out of other people's way. Bramble rash, getting out of the way of fast bike riders and walkers coming at you two, three, even four abreast was a regular feature! Both of us 'muttered' at times. Being essentially on the same wavelength, we suffered from no interpersonal problems, a subject much discussed by the media. And we kept ourselves largely mentally 'intact' too, but Christobel at times felt tearful, not an unusual event we found and I, during the middle of the last full lockdown, let it 'get to me' too, finding myself feeling exceedingly melancholic at times. I was reminded of words made by Mr Bennett in Jane Austen's *Pride and Prejudice*, when talking to his two eldest girls about the costs incurred by the folly of his youngest daughter, I said to my mate, "It'll pass, it'll pass…"

It wasn't until the end of March we broke free…an easing of regulations allowing more people to meet, outside and for me, sailing aboard a cabined craft, which I wrote about in the two earlier chapters.

Then in late May, a further reduction in restrictions was made in England and the other UK nations with varying differences…We were allowed away sailing which broke the growing monotony of daily walks with little else to look forward to.

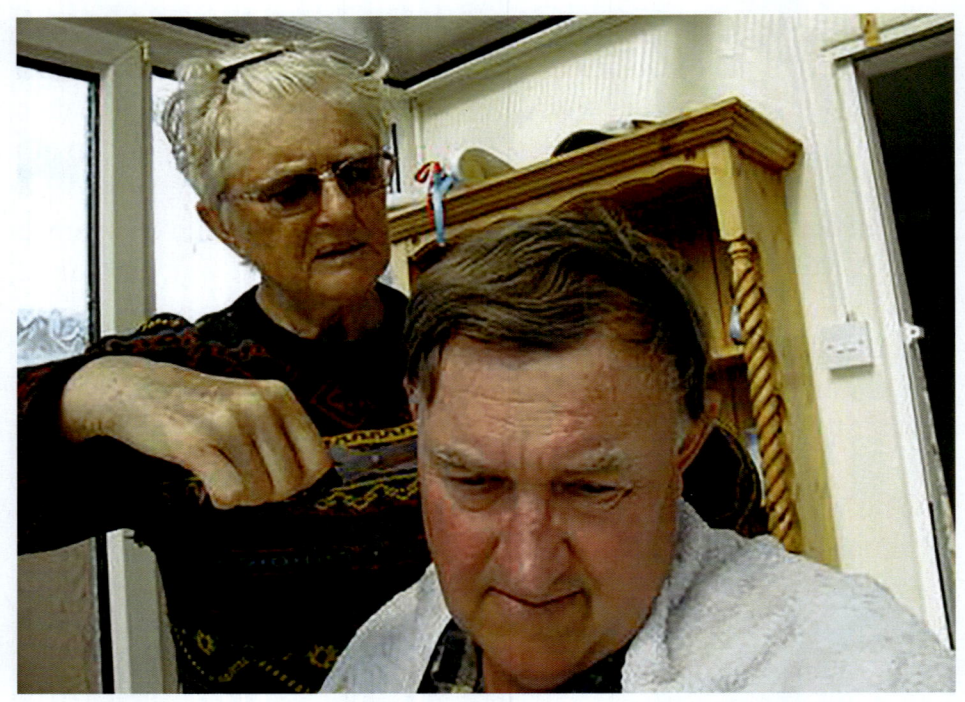

The author has a lockdown hair trim. Note his wife's hair clip!

Summer arrived with another further easing as vaccination levels rose above a stated 75% of the eligible population. However, round the world, many countries previously less affected felt a fuller impact and it was clear to us as it was to the health experts, none of us would be 'safe' until everyone was vaccinated. It would be a long process. It must be remembered, 'Man' has only managed to properly defeat just one disease, Smallpox.

Even, with a rising number of new variant cases, hospitalisation remained relatively 'low' as were deaths, thank goodness. People, though, were beginning to think it was all over, palpably noticeable when shopping especially in large stores. Frightening to a point.

Scientists said the Covid-19 virus will not just disappear. As if to remind us all, new strains, or variants as they're termed, have continued to appear, as if time-tabled, to trouble the world with uncomfortable periods while scientists studied them. Covid's effects on the human population will surely diminish with vaccination and like other problems, we'll surely have to learn to live with it. As 2021 faded and 2022 began, another covid variant took off and spread. That was Omicron, with its own mutation, Omicon-2. The world held its collective breath. Thankfully it was soon found, if caught, vaccinated people generally only had what was described as cold-like symptoms. The unvaccinated, well, sadly they did not fare so well. The latter must be a lesson, surely. By the spring of 2022, much of the world was well into reverting to a new normality of careful watchfulness.

An abiding memory I shall keep was of the opening week of the first UK wide lockdown in March 2020. We had not 'caught on' about what was happening in the outside world greatly, keeping ourselves to ourselves. The first lockdown Friday came round and we went off shopping, as usual. Both of us were aghast at the long queues with barriers feeding people shop-wards. Upon finally getting inside, many of the items on our weekly list were unobtainable. Shelves had been stripped bare. It was total madness. We needed simple things like loo paper, flour, a packet of pasta and the restocking of used cleaning products. There was none of these items left! Our loo paper problem was solved by initially collecting some from *Whimbrel*!

Soon after, there was an impassioned plea from a nurse, deeply tired and severely stressed after another long hard shift on a Covid ward. At breaking point, with tears streaming down her face, she asked people to think of others. To think of those who can't queue for ages during the day 'cos they're on watch. It was heart-rending. One didn't need any imagination to feel her fright and frustration. It was palpable. It was a very moving and sad reflection on our society. We're in it together was the slogan. 'No, we're bloody well not...' that was clear.

A whole year was 'lost' to us all. For many, the loss was extremely personal, especially if 'detailed off' to isolate oneself from society. It meant a total reliance on others and planning – finding a slot – for grocery deliveries.

Thankfully, we came through unscathed. Well, nearly anyway, but after a west-country holiday following the winter 2022 lockdown, we both succumbed, lightly, thankfully! Sadly, however, like hundreds of thousands across the world, a near neighbour of ours succumbed early on. They must all be remembered.

Whatever their creed, God Bless them all.

What did or do I feel? Wiser, certainly. Thankful? Yes, exceedingly. Thank God. "What more can one say…" I mouthed, smiling thinly: I couldn't help feeling huge sorrow too.

Sailing alone, homebound, across the Thames highway from Kent to Essex in the autumn of 2021, I remembered a looming blood test for my six-monthly prostate check. I smiled gratefully as I gazed in awe at a powerful glowing dawn illuminating the sky. It filled me with such joy and hopefulness. I wanted to share it with the boat's mate, Christobel, who would have so loved it too. That growing light, I thought, was such a powerful reminder of life…

A dawn for living life…

So, wiser and with far greater respect for the frailties of life, I shall, as said before, continue taking the best of what is offered and deal with the rotten remainder, as well as I can. And, with my dear mate beside me for many more years to come, I shall continue, as I said to my radiographer, 'Sailing through life…'

Bibliography and Further Reading

Allen, Grant, *The Tidal Thames,* (London: Cassell & Co, Ltd, 1892)

Ardley, Nick, *Mudlarking Thames Estuary Cruising Yarns,* (Stroud: Amberley Publishing, 2010)

Ardley, Nick, *Rochester to Richmond, A Thames Estuary Sailor's View*, Fonthill Media, 2017

Ardley, Nick, *Salt Marsh & Mud A Year's Sailing on the Thames Estuary,* (Stroud: Amberley publishing, 2009)

Ardley, Nick, Swinging the Lamp, Thames Estuary Tidal Tales, Fonthill Media, 2016

Ardley, Nick, *The Jottings of a Thames Estuary Ditch-crawler,* (Stroud, Amberley publishing, 2011)

Ardley, Nick, *The May Flower A Barging Childhood,* (Stroud, Tempus 2007, reprinted The History Press, 2010)

Carr, Frank G. G. *Sailing Barges*, Rev Ed 1951, Peter Davies, London

Church, Richard, *Kent,* Robert Hale Ltd, 1948

Hoskins, W. G., *The making of the English landscape*, Little Toller Books, 2013 (First pub 1955)

Jessup, Ronald & Frank, The Cinque Ports, Batsford Ltd, London, 1952

Maxwell, Donald, *Unknown Kent*, Bodley Head Ltd, 1921

Muir Evans, H., *A Short History of the Thames Estuary*, Imray, Laurie, Norrie & Wilson, London, 1940

Perks, Richard-Hugh, *George Bargebrick – The story of George Smeed the brick and cement king*, Meresborough Books, 1981

Papers:
Jill Eddison, *Developments in the Lower Rother Valleys up to 1600*, Academic Journal Offprint from – Archaeologia Cantiana 102, 1985. (Public access from various sources)

Web sites of interest:
www.nationalhistoricships.org.uk/register/618/primrose
www.ryesown.co.uk/the-marsh-barges/
www.villagenet.co.uk – Changing face of Romney Marsh
www.wikipedia.org/wiki/Rhee_Wall
www.wikipedia.org/wiki/Smallhythe_Place